Advance Praise for

Jeanie Shaw courageously and insightfully engages one of the most important contemporary challenges of our time, especially for those of us connected to the Restoration Movement. How shall we read the Bible in ways that are faithful to its message and provide space for the Spirit to form us into the image of Christ? Recognizing the relative poverty of historic approaches within the Restoration Movement, she draws on various perspectives to invite us to read the Bible anew, attentive not only to its historical and theological meaning but also its formative function as a moment where we encounter God.

—John Mark Hicks, Retired Professor of Theology,
Lipscomb University

A serious study of the way we have interpreted the Bible in the Stone-Campbell Restoration Movement and more particularly in the International Churches of Christ is long overdue. I am grateful for Jeanie Shaw who has carefully tackled this challenging but vital issue, showing how some of our old paradigms stunted our spiritual growth, and offering a more Jesus-centered and transformational hermeneutic. This can be a game-changing book.

—Tom A. Jones, author, teacher, former editor DPI

In this carefully researched and deeply insightful work, Jeanie Shaw shows how understanding scripture as a pattern to be reproduced inhibits the development of a healthy unitive spirituality. Following a survey of the roots of pattern theology, Shaw gives examples of how that approach to scripture distorts the image of God and blocks healthy spiritual formation. She then suggests using three other "lenses," each of which retains pattern theology's commitment to scripture but adds missing spiritual insights. The theological lens focuses on the character and work of God rather than how to do things; the Redemptive Movement lens centers on the historical movement of the Spirit toward God's ultimate ethic; and the Spirit Hermeneutic emphasizes experiencing the work of and being taught by God's Spirit in scripture.

In the end, Shaw calls for an experiential spiritual approach to scripture that forms followers of Jesus in the healthy spirituality we are meant to receive and thrive in, and which alone can bring the unity Christ prayed for among his followers. This engaging study provides Christians with rich resources for healthy spiritual formation rooted in scripture.

—Douglas A. Foster, Professor of Church History Emeritus, Graduate School of Theology, Abilene Christian University

Jeanie writes about the basic subject of how we are supposed to read and understand the Bible in a manner that changes our lives, the church, and the world. Yet, most in our family of churches have little idea of what correct interpretation should involve, and even less knowledge of our history as a part of the Restoration Movement with its patternistic interpretative approach. She exposes concerning issues in a courageous way. She not only addresses principles, but includes current examples among us that will be welcomed by those who love truth. Kudos to her for her fearless approach in addressing a subject that has needed to be addressed among us for decades!

—Gordon Ferguson, author, teacher, former Director of the Asia-Pacific Leadership Academy and Ukraine Institute of Ministry

Re-Examining Our Lenses:

The Relationship Between
Restoration Movement Hermeneutics
and Spiritual Formation

Jeanie Shaw

Rexamining Our Lenses: The Relationship Between Restoration Movement Hermeneutics and Spiritual Formation

Printed in the United States of America.

ISBN: 978-1-958723-25-8.

Unless otherwise indicated, all Scripture references are from the Holy Bible, New International Version, copyright 1973, 1978, 1984, 2011 by the International Bible Society. Used by permission of Zondervan Bible Publishers.

Cover design by Roy Appalsamy and interior layout by Toney Mulhollan. The text face is set in Calluna and Myriad Pro.

Theatron Press titles may be purchased in bulk for classroom instruction.

Theatron Press is committed to caring wisely for God's creation and uses recycled paper whenever possible.

About the author: **Jeanie Shaw** is a teacher and communicator of spiritual growth. She received her Master's in Christian Spirituality and Formation from Regent University and her Doctorate in Spiritual Formation and Discipleship from Nazarene Theological Seminary. She serves as a Christian life coach, teacher, and spiritual director. She finds great joy in journeying alongside others, helping them discover God's presence as they navigate life's joys and challenges. Jeanie recently retired after serving for over four decades in full-time ministry, alongside her late husband. She considers her work with the underserved, particularly with orphans in Eastern Europe, a deeply formative part of her life. She resides in New England, enjoying close proximity to her four adult children and eight grandchildren, whom she adores. You can learn more about her ministry at riverfrontcoaching.com.

Theatron Press is an imprint of
Illumination Publishers International

Contents

Acknowledgments

I began the research for this book both during and following my husband's illness and passing from this physical life. His belief in me, and the expression of his desire to see me accomplish my dream of further theological education inspired me when nights were long and my living room overflowed with books. His life and memory call me to continually learn while seeking the unity of the Spirit as I continue to live life. In his absence, my adult children have spurred me on with their encouragement throughout this writing process. Thank you.

I also wish to acknowledge several teachers in my church tradition who have believed in me throughout my academic journey, respectfully engaging me in numerous theological discussions while offering their years of experience as teachers and church leaders. Thank you, Gordon Ferguson and Tom A. Jones. Also, Dr. John Mark Hicks, an expert in the field of my study, has patiently reviewed my work and offered valuable input and encouragement along the way. He was invaluable in helping me find a clearer lens for viewing Scripture. Thank you.

My doctoral professors and cohort, with their keen insights and genuine care, have continually fanned into flame my desire to grow and learn. Several "grass-roots" spiritual formation discussion groups within my family of churches have encouraged me, as well as the Common Grounds Unity initiative within the Restoration Movement churches.

I thank God for groups such as these and for individuals who seek the unity for which Jesus prayed in John 17. As I learn to view life as part of God's story weaved throughout the Scriptures and better understand the lenses through which I view Scripture, my desire for us to become one as Jesus and the Father are one continually grows.

Introduction

When I was in my early twenties, a relative engaged me in conversation, asking me if I thought he was going to hell. He sought to follow Jesus, as did I, but he belonged to a different "Bible-believing" church, thus was suspect. Though I told him that only the Scriptures could judge him, my views, based on perceived patterns of commands, examples, and inferences I interpreted from the Scriptures left little room for discussion. I was stuck in my hermeneutic (the way I interpret Scripture), even though I had no understanding of the word or its meaning. He then asked me if I knew when my church began, and without hesitation I replied, "It began on the day of Pentecost." He asked me questions about Alexander Campbell, of whom I knew nothing. I mistakenly told him that no man, apart from Jesus, had any influence on the beginnings of my church. Though we might still hold some interpretive differences, how I wish I had known my church's history and employed clearer lenses of biblical interpretation to guide my heart toward a deeper understanding and practice of mercy over judgment, grace over performance, unity over boundaries, and relationship over observance, qualities essential to healthy spiritual formation. Instead, my hermeneutic encouraged my formation toward the unChristlike postures of judgment over mercy, boundaries over unity, and observance over relationship.

The profound relationship between interpretation and spiritual formation must be recognized and explored. Spiritual formation often implies the practice of spiritual disciplines, but it involves much more. Ruth Haley Barton defines spiritual formation as the "process by which Christ is formed in us for the glory of God, for the abundance of our own lives, and the sake of others."[1] My nuanced version defines it as "beholding God, as revealed through the incarnate Christ, with increasing clarity and giving Him the space to, through His indwelling Spirit, transform us more closely into His image, thus reflecting Him in our daily

---

lives and relationships."[2] I believe our formation begins with the ways we view God and the Scriptures.

My Christian background is deeply rooted in the Restoration Movement (RM), also known as the Stone-Campbell Movement, and will be my reference for examining this relationship, particularly within the stream of the RM to which I belong, the International Churches of Christ (ICOC). While this is my context, I believe this relationship between our interpretation and spiritual formation has far-reaching implications and applications to other streams, though my focus is on those within the RM churches. I believe our churches need a lens adjustment that considers our historical biases and incorporates adjusted lenses leading to healthier spiritual formation, thus resulting in greater unity.

It has been said that we learn from history that we don't learn from history.[3] Thus, our churches need increased knowledge of RM history, an understanding of its hermeneutic, and a hermeneutical lens adjustment that fosters deeper spiritual transformation. Members of RM churches certainly cannot learn from their history when it is not taught to leaders or members. There also remains a void in hermeneutical training among both RM leaders and members, hindering them from knowledge of inconsistencies and presuppositions in their (our) interpretative methods. Such teaching and training could better equip both leaders and members to reframe their hermeneutic toward a more Christ-focused and Spirit-led interpretation of Scripture, thus becoming more deeply formed into the likeness of Christ.

My desire to study and write on this topic springs from my observation of a blurred hermeneutical process—my own, and that of my church. I have been in RM churches all my life. I became a Christian when I was thirteen years old and served in the ministry in the Church of Christ and the ICOC from my college graduation in 1975, until I retired from women's ministry in 2021. Over the past decade, I (and my church) faced new questions con-

---

2. Since I am often asked about spiritual formation, I sought to employ a definition that more fully includes the Trinitarian involvement in our spiritual transformation and decreases an emphasis on practices.

3. The quote attributed to George Santayanas reads, "Those who cannot learn from history are bound to repeat it."

cerning biblical interpretation. In addition to these questions, the racial unrest in the United States over the past few years prompted me to further educate myself concerning the history and continued presence of racism in the United States. I was mortified to learn of a more deeply entrenched systemic racism of which I was previously unaware. The American history I was taught left out many dreadful, historical realities.

Similarly, I feared that a lack of understanding of my own church history and hermeneutics created unintentional and unknown blind spots. This realization coincided with my three-year study on the role of women in the church. From this study, I learned how my deeply engrained hermeneutic had affected my understandings, presuppositions, and perspectives of certain scriptures. I could no longer reconcile some things I had been previously taught with what I was now learning, and I began to question the selective literalism interpretive method in patternism (the Restoration Movement's default way to interpret Scripture) that I often observed in my church's doctrine and practice. I came to realize our hermeneutic took some scriptures at face value as commands, apostolic examples to follow today, and inferences leading to strict conclusions while explaining others as temporary and cultural, sometimes even within the same chapter of the Bible.[4] The subjective conclusions viewed from examples or inferences varied, depending on whatever the espouser deemed as the "biblical pattern," This method of interpretation became known as patternism.

As a result of my studies, I wrote a book about women in the church.[5] Though I thoroughly vetted it with numerous ICOC

---

4. Patterns taken from 1 Corinthians 14 prohibited women from speaking, while earlier in the chapter they were prophesying. The wearing of veils, prohibition for braided hair and gold, and practice of holy kisses are not applied today though women not speaking in the assembly has often been applied. Polygamy, levirate, and primogeniture practices are considered cultural, yet the patriarchal system is often viewed as a biblical pattern to be followed. I encountered questions I had been afraid to ask. Since I hold a high view of Scripture, I felt that questioning would be near-blasphemous. I wondered why some OT (and NT) acts of disobedience were punished by death and other recorded acts of disobedience were not punished. I realized that even if one had complete faith that their loved one would be healed and called upon the elders for prayer and anointing, their loved one still died. I had to wrestle with such questions which led me to a different, redemptive, theological, and narrative way to read Scripture while still holding it in the highest regard.

5. Jeanie Shaw, *The View From Paul's Window: Paul's Teachings on Women* (Spring, TX: Illumination Publishers, 2020).

leaders, some in my home church strongly resisted its publication. Out of respect for their concerns, I delayed the publication for two years, until more conversations could take place. Also, during that time, the pandemic of 2020 brought increased opportunities for people to hear from online pulpits beyond their own church settings. Curious church members, with the click of a keyboard or phone, garnered other views among Christendom and began to question some of their own church practices. As a result, I noticed more of our church's youth asking questions over social media, "deconstructing" their belief systems and hermeneutics and some leaving the church of their youth.

While some of our church's campus and young adult ministries are thriving, many young adults have walked away, and overall, our membership is decreasing. The ICOC (and mainline churches of Christ) lost many millennials who grew up in the church,[6] and numerous Gen Z's whose parents are members are not becoming members. Few members of the RM have any significant understanding of RM church history or its prominent hermeneutic, because these have not been taught. Furthermore, our churches have been largely unsuccessful in maintaining unity in diversity. To address these problems, I argue the importance of the relationship between our hermeneutic and spiritual formation.

My church's preferred hermeneutic has many great attributes, but it can also negatively affect formation. A look back at RM voices of the past, along with current voices, becomes necessary to navigate ways forward. I will first highlight significant voices of the past and their interpretations of Scripture, showing ways their hermeneutic affected their formation and ways this "pattern" continues today. While some available literature addresses the pattern hermeneutic, none have studied its effect on formation.

The Pattern Voices: Learning from the few resources on the topic

Professor John Mark Hicks of Lipscomb University serves

---

6. This age group is our smallest, as can be seen in church memberships databases and demographics represented in conference registrations.

as the most prolific author addressing the effects of the pattern hermeneutic employed in the Restoration Movement. His recent book and various articles explore the RM's history of patternism, and his most recent book explores the women's role viewed from both a patternistic and theological hermeneutic.[7] F. LaGard Smith, a professor of law and editor of *The Narrated Bible* and *The Daily Bible,* whose views I further explore in chapter three, remains a strong proponent of the pattern hermeneutic, authoring several books in support of patternism and limited roles for women.[8] While several RM professors and teachers, including Richard Hughes and Douglas Foster, have written the most recent and thorough accounts of RM history,[9] little has been written on the history of the International Churches of Christ (ICOC). C. Foster Stanback published a book on the history of the ICOC in 2005,[10] and in 2007, Thomas A. Jones wrote a historical memoir of his life in the ICOC. [11] Gordon Ferguson also included some history of the ICOC in his recent memoir,[12] and David Pocta wrote an article entitled "Kip McKean: Saint or Scoundrel," published in the new academic journal, *Teleios.*[13] Roger Lamb, former editor of "Disciples Today," the news website for the ICOC, gathered ICOC historical documents in a recently published collection on the "Disciples Today" website.[14] Throughout this book, I will make

---

7. Hicks two most recent books are *Searching for the Pattern: My Journey in Interpreting the Bible* (Nashville, TN: John Mark Hicks, 2019) and *Women Serving God: My Journey in Understanding Their Story in the Bible* (Nashville, TN: John Mark Hicks, 2020).

8. F. LaGard Smith wrote *What Most Women Want* (Eugene, OR: Harvest House, 1992), and *Male Spiritual Leadership* (Nashville, TN: 20th Century Christian, 1998).

9. Richard T Hughes wrote *Reviving the Ancient Faith: The Story of Churches of Christ in America* (Abilene, TX: ACU Press, 2008), and Douglas A. Foster wrote *A Life of Alexander Campbell* (Grand Rapids, MI: Eerdmans, 2020).

10. C. Foster Stanback, *Into All Nations: A History of the International Churches of Christ* (Spring, TX: Illumination Publishers, 2005).

11. Thomas A. Jones, *In Search of a City: An Autobiographical Perspective on a Remarkable but Controversial Movement* (Spring Hill, TN: DPI, 2007).

12. Gordon Ferguson, *My Three Lives: A Story of One Man and Three Movements* (Spring, TX: Illumination Publishers, 2016).

13. David Pocta, "Thomas Wayne 'Kip' McKean: Saint or Scoundrel-Normalizing Perspectives on a Foundational Figure in the International Church of Christ," *Teleios: A Journal to Promote Holistic Christian Spirituality,* vol. 1, no 2 (2021), 43-62.

14. https://icochistory.org/.

mention of contributions from the small amount of RM literature that relates to this topic.

There are currently no writings on the relationship between patternism and spiritual formation in the RM churches, with the exception of a few paragraphs from Douglas Foster and David Pocta in a recent *Teleios* journal publication.[15] Therefore, there is a lacuna in the scholarship, which I hope to fill.

My Intent

Throughout this book, I explore ways the founders of the Restoration Movement interpreted Scripture and how their methodology and practice affected spiritual formation in the church from then until today. When interpretation created static dogma, as it often did, deforming spiritual practices followed, including the desire to dominate. This caused and continues to encourage disunity. I believe that recognizing and reframing the far-reaching "rules" and church traditions deeply rooted within pattern theology will better encourage spiritual formation, resulting in greater unity.

Even though the Bible does not give the answers to all Bible questions, the pattern hermeneutic, or method of interpreting the scriptures, leaves little room for discussion, as it quickly discounts and counters "off-pattern" views, labeling them as unsound doctrine. Spiritual formation, which by its definition assumes change, must facilitate and encourage further discussions and teachings to foster greater unity, a necessary goal of transformation into the image of Christ.

Throughout this book I will seek to answer the questions:

- How has the deep-rooted Restoration Movement history and hermeneutic formed our default biblical interpretation? (I will use the term "hermeneutic" throughout this book. It refers to the theories and methods we use to interpret Scripture.)

---

15. Douglas Foster, "The Stone Campbell Movement and the International Churches of Christ," *Teleios: A Journal to Promote Holistic Christian Spirituality*, vol. 1, no 2 (2021), 38, and David Pocta, "Thomas Wayne 'Kip' McKean: Saint or Scoundrel," *Teleios* (2021), 57-58.

- How does this hermeneutic inform and continue to influence spiritual formation?

- How can we adjust and reframe our interpretation to better include God's redemptive love and the leading of the living Spirit of God?

- How can my church tradition more effectively teach people to engage the Spirit of God, thus becoming more comfortable with uncertainty, mystery, and experience?

- How can a revised hermeneutic help us achieve unity without uniformity?

Throughout the chapters, I answer the five questions posed. In chapter one, I recount a brief history of the Restoration Movement along with its reliance on patternism. I analyze the profound impact of the pattern hermeneutic on spiritual formation through exploration of the history of the RM and its leaders from its inception until today. I next explore ways this interpretive method of the RM informs, forms, and deforms one's reflection of Christ and relationships with one another.

In chapter two, I focus on the effects of the pattern hermeneutic on my church tradition, the International Churches of Christ (ICOC). While these effects are found in other RM streams, I use interviews from recognized teachers within my church to explore the effects of the pattern hermeneutic on church practice and formation among our churches. Healthy interpretation calls for distinction between "the baby" and "the bathwater" in the RM interpretive method, and I shall analyze both the good and bad tendencies seen in patternism. Some who hold a pattern hermeneutic fear that interpreting the Scriptures through new lenses, or engaging with culture (whether ancient Near Eastern or present-day) will weaken biblical integrity by straying from the biblical pattern. I explore such fear, and suggest several ways to counter the negative impact that patternism can have on our theology, discipleship, evangelism, and unity by suggesting adjustments to our hermeneutical lenses.

In chapter three, I offer adjustments to the RM's one-dimensional hermeneutical lens, exploring several interpretive lenses that can enhance spiritual formation in our fellowship: the theological lens, as explained by John Mark Hicks; the redemptive/trajectory lens offered by William Webb, and the Spirit Hermeneutic suggested by Craig Keener. Using a widely interpreted passage of Scripture, I show ways these lenses affect both interpretation and formation.

In chapter four, I explore ways that the pattern hermeneutic minimizes the working of the Spirit of God, often resulting in an anemic spiritual and relational experience among members. I offer ways that relational experiences can further inform the reason-based interpretation of Scripture currently employed in the pattern hermeneutic, and thus strengthen spiritual formation.

Lastly, in chapter five I go "back to the future" through writings of several early restoration leaders, noting their broader, less dogmatic hermeneutic that advanced their case for unity without uniformity and resulted in greater church growth and healthier formation. I urge a more accurate teaching of our church history and of the pattern hermeneutic to inform and nudge our church culture toward a more grace-filled, loving, and experiential spiritual formation.

The Restoration Movement's pattern hermeneutic, though practiced in varying degrees in our churches, continues to impact its members' individual and communal formation. The unity between different streams of RM churches has been difficult at best. By employing a theological, redemptive, Spirit-led hermeneutic, I believe our members can more closely reflect the image of Christ, allowing unity (in diversity) to become more of a reality among the Restoration Movement churches.

CHAPTER ONE

Restoration Movement History: Hermeneutics and Its Effect on Formation

We can hold to the illusion that what has come before has no impact on us, but of course this is nonsense; the imagination and practices that mobilize our lives are delivered to us on the undercurrents of a particular history.[16]

The Restoration Movement, founded in the late eighteenth and early nineteenth centuries to bring unity among Christians from Protestant Reformation denominations, relied on a method of interpreting Scripture known as patternism. Restoration leaders, who believed a return to the pattern or "blueprint" of the primitive church could unite all Protestants, searched the Scriptures for direct commands, examples, and necessary inferences, speaking where the Bible speaks and remaining silent where the Bible was silent.[17] Sadly, instead of the noble purpose intended, over the years the RM experienced division as leaders fought for control, practiced condescending attitudes, and exhibited pride and quickness to condemn. The profound impact of the pattern hermeneutic on spiritual formation can be traced through appeals and publications of leaders throughout the history of the movement as their dreams of unity became nightmares of divisions. Too often, leaders' ecclesial perfectionism, derived from their pattern hermeneutic, resulted in harmful formation as compared with others, whose more grace-filled hermeneutic resulted in healthier spiritual formation. These contrasts highlight ways

---

16. Andrew Root, *Faith Formation in a Secular Age* (Grand Rapids, MI: Baker Academics, 2017), xxi.

17. Patternism was not a new hermeneutic begun by Restoration leaders. Zwingli practiced patternism, as did Calvinists and Puritans from the seventeenth century. Campbell had Presbyterian roots. Also, Edward Dering (1540-1576), offered one of the earliest comments on commands, examples, and inferences, insisting that biblical conclusions were drawn from "proportion, or deduction, by consequence... is as well the Word of God as that which is express commandment or example." Quoted by Theodore Dwight Bozeman, *To Live Ancient Lives: The Primitivist Dimension in Puritanism* (Chapel Hill, NC: University of North Carolina Press, 1988), 70.

the deeply-rooted hermeneutical trends continue to impact formation in RM churches.

Appeals for Restoration

When explaining differences between the Restoration Movement and the earlier Reformation Movement, several Restoration preachers of the twentieth century used an analogy of a crashed car.[18] The owner of a crashed car does not want their car reformed; instead, they wish it restored to its original state. This analogy tells Restoration church members that the desired outcome for biblical Christianity is restoration rather than reformation. Restoration leaders taught that Reformers only changed some existing church traditions, falling short of restoring primitive Christianity. Restoration leaders presented their views of a more accurate interpretation of Scripture to restore New Testament Christianity. In 1825, Alexander Campbell penned this distinction of restoration versus reformation:

A restoration of the ancient order of things is all that is necessary to the happiness and usefulness of christians (sic). No attempt "to reform the doctrine, discipline and government of the church," (a phrase too long in use,) can promise a better result than those which have been attempted and languished to death. We are glad to see, in the above extract, that the thing proposed, is to bring christianity and the church of the present day up to the standard of the New Testament. This is in substance, though in other terms, what we contend for. To bring the societies of christians up to the New Testament, is just to bring the disciples individually and collectively, to walk in the faith, and in the commandments of the Lord and Saviour, as presented in that blessed volume; and this is to restore the ancient order of things. Celebrated as the era of reformation is, we doubt not but that the era of restoration will as far transcend it in importance and fame, through the long and blissful Millennium, as the New Testament transcends in simplicity, beauty, excellency, and majesty, the dogmas and notions of the creed of Westminster and the canons of the Assembly's Digest. Just in so far as the ancient order of things, or the religion of the New Testament, is restored, just so far has the Millennium commenced, and so far

---

18. This was recounted in some individual Bible studies and sermon notes, discovered from the notes of a long-time elder in the Church of Christ.

have its blessings been enjoyed. For to the end of time, we shall have no other revelation of the Spirit, no other New Testament, no other Saviour, and no other religion than we now have, when we understand, believe and practice the doctrine of Christ delivered to us by his apostles.[19]

Campbell appealed for a different, uniting approach to interpretation by restoring the ancient order of things as defined by the New Testament. Though denominational doctrines and creeds were commonplace in Protestantism, such appeals can be traced back many centuries.

Early appeals
Appeals to return to the primitive scriptures started long before the Restoration Movement. Though they would not be labeled "restorationists," Patristic fathers first spoke of plans to unite Christians by restoring the primitive scriptures. Tertullian (second century CE) warned of Greek heresy clouding biblical interpretation, and Montanus sought to build congregations to primitive piety.[20] The fourth century Nicaean Council convened to address departures from the faith, though Restoration leaders would consider such proclamations as extrabiblical creeds, adding tradition and dogma beyond the Scriptures. The RM leaders taught, "There is one 'Divine Creed'—many 'Human Creeds'... The trouble arises from the fact that men incorporate their opinions and speculations in their formal creeds, and 'teach for doctrines the commandments of men.'"[21] This assumes that men's speculations do not enter into views of commands, examples, and inferences, which is a poor assumption.

In the same century as the Nicaean Council, Priscillian called for a return to apostolic practice, resulting in persecution and the destruction of most of his writings by the Catholic church. From

---

19. Alexander Campbell, "A Restoration of the Ancient Order of Things, No. I" *The Christian Baptist*, Vol. 2. Number 7 (1825): 124-8.   https://webfiles.acu.edu/departments/Library/HR/restmov_nov11/www.mun.ca/rels/restmov/texts/acampbell/tcb/TCB207.HTM#Essay2.

20. James DeForest Murch, *Christians Only: A History of the Restoration Movement* (Cincinnati, OH: Standard Publishing, 1963), 10.

21. George A. Klingman, *Church History for Busy People* (Nashville, TN: Gospel Advocate Co, 1960), 48.

the seventh to ninth centuries, a group known as the Paulicians sought to maintain the primitive faith.[22]

Fourteenth century theologian John Wycliffe taught the importance of "Scripture alone," and Czech theologian John Huss called for a return to Scripture which eventually resulted in his martyrdom. The sixteenth-century Anabaptists sounded the call to restore the primitive church, particularly in a return to baptism by immersion. The Anabaptists, with their plea and commitment to radically restore biblical doctrine and practice, are considered the first to fit the description of the Restorationists, though many others set the stage.

The early Restoration leaders' noble desire for unity in Protestantism gave way to a hermeneutic that made unity difficult, if not impossible. John Mark Hicks explains:

> While Luther's question was primarily, "Where can I find the merciful God?," Zwingli's [Zurich Reformation leader] question was basically, "Where can I find the true church?" The search for the true church became a search for models, examples, and commands within the New Testament that would provide a pattern, and only those congregations that conformed to the pattern were true churches. This agenda generated the Puritan movement in England, and the most radical of the Puritans were the Separatists.[23]

While Reformers sought the return to patristic interpretation of Scripture, the Restoration leaders would contest interpretations which they believed veered from Scripture's specific commands, examples, and necessary inferences. They believed the Reformers' dogmas and creeds led to the fragmented, denominational nature of Christendom.

Protestantism faced challenges in the eighteenth century as Voltaire and the age of reason brought decreased credibility to Scripture and a sharp decline in church membership. This challenge led Christian leaders in the 1800s to the Great Awakening.

---

22. Murch, *Christians Only*, 11.

23. John Mark Hicks, "Searching for the Pattern," *Teleios: A Journal to Promote Holistic Christian Spirituality*, Vol. 5, No 1 (2023): 75.

The Wesleyan revival, Yale President Dwight's sermon, "The Nature and Danger of Infidel Philosophy," and James McGready's persuasive preaching against humanism brought exponential growth to Protestantism.[24]

Reports from this period noted Christians worshipping together without the addition of any name other than "Christian."[25] The journal *Advocate and Messenger* reported "we mean to be New Testament Christians, without any sectarian name connected with it, without sectarian creeds, articles, confessions, or discipline to illuminate the Scriptures."[26] These calls back to Scripture set the stage for men who would become leaders of the Restoration Movement, a movement seeking to recreate the New Testament church through rejection of creeds and viewing themselves as "Christians only." A widely distributed church tract of the mid-twentieth century, authored by Batsell Barrett Baxter, explains this firmly held conviction over the years:

> The church of Christ is neither Catholic, Protestant, nor Jewish. We are uniquely different for we are endeavoring to go all the way back to the original New Testament church. Using the New Testament as our blueprint we have re-established in the twentieth century Christ's church. It fits no modern label. It is not just another denomination.[27]

Baxter's summary sought to both define the church of Christ's desire for non-denominational status and to document its blueprint, or pattern, hermeneutic.

Restoration Movement Founding Fathers

Because the Restoration Movement resisted identification as a denomination or sect, most members of churches whose roots trace back to the founders know little to nothing about

---

24. Murch, *Christians Only,* 23, 28, 31. McGready was part of the Second Awakening.

25. "Christians only" was a term used is the Elias Smith and Abner Jones' Christian Connexion Movement and in other small groups like James O'Kelly's Republican Methodists.

26. *Advocate and Messenger,* 1827, cited in Murch, *Christians Only,* 33.

27. Batsell Barret Baxter and Carroll Ellis, *Neither Catholic, Protestant, Nor Jew* (Nashville: Hillsboro Church of Christ, n.d.), 12.

the founders' hermeneutics, teachings, and personal lives nor do they connect the predominant hermeneutic as significant to their spiritual formation.[28] Today, families can learn of their roots through DNA companies such as Ancestry.com. Similarly, an understanding of Restoration Movement roots can shed light on some of its inherited tendencies, strengths, and weaknesses. One way we understand the inherited tendencies of the Restoration Movement comes from observing ways the leaders understood Scripture apart from tradition. Their formative tendencies can also be discerned from their publications and writings, their rational, empirical, and pragmatic methods of interpretation, and their de-emphasis on the Old Testament.

History attributes the founding of this movement to Thomas Campbell, his son, Alexander, and Barton Stone. In 1809, Thomas Campbell, from a Scottish Presbyterian background, penned the independent publication *Declaration and Address,* programmatic for what would later be termed "the Restoration Movement." He pled for cooperation among existing Christian denominations and coined the phrase, "Where the Scriptures speak, we speak; and where the Scriptures are silent, we are silent."[29] His insistence that the way to peace and unity was through conformity to the teachings of the Scriptures became complicated, as ways to interpret Scripture widely vary according to one's presupposed views and hermeneutical lenses.

Thomas Campbell assumed that matters concerning salvation were clear enough that readers will reach the same conclusion. He emphasized that differences of opinion would not be made tests of fellowship and warned against division among Christians, calling it anti-Christian, anti-scriptural, and unnatural. He believed the apostles stand on the same plain of infallibility and authority in their teaching as Jesus.[30] His desire for unity included a high value he placed on piety.

28. Churches of Christ, Disciples of Christ (Christian Church), and the Christian Church/Churches of Christ trace their roots to the Stone-Campbell Restoration Movement.

29. Murch, *Christians Only,* 40.

30. Thomas Campbell, "Declaration and Address," in Alexander Campbell, Barton W. Stone, Thomas Campbell, Isaac Errett, J.H. Garrison, *Historical Documents Advocation Christian Union: The Restoration Movement Library* (US: Cobb Publishing, 2017), 41.

Publications' wars of words

Campbell stressed the necessity of moral character. Sadly, his noble proposition would soon erode through "positioning wars" among journals and periodicals. Restoration leaders who proposed one right way to interpret scriptures concerning the practice of sacraments and proper worship conduct would soon become dogmatic when expressing their views, showcasing ways all people interpret Scripture with their own systems and presuppositions.

Seeking to address varying interpretations, Thomas penned:

> A second evil is, not only judging our brother to be absolutely wrong, because he differs from our opinions, but more especially, our judging him to be a transgressor of the law in so doing, and, of course, treating him as such by censuring or otherwise exposing him to contempt, or, at least, preferring ourselves before him in our own judgement, saying, as it were, 'Stand by, I am holier than thou.'[31]

Sadly, within one generation character vices reared their ugly heads. That which began as an appeal for unity degraded into petty divisions.

A gifted preacher and prolific writer who did not fear conflict, Thomas' son, Alexander, further carried his and his father's shared convictions through powerful preaching, debates, and publications. Alexander published The *Millennial Harbinger*, to promote a return to New Testament Christianity. The title reflected Campbell's belief in the millennial return of Christ, thus *Millennial Harbinger* announces the coming of the millennium. Alexander's positions, addressed through his publications, wavered throughout his life, at times promoting principles that seemed to justify exclusivism while at other times his articles brought accusations of ecumenicism. Though he sought compassion and equality, his nationalistic pride and belief in America's superiority reinforced his belief in the myth of Anglo-Saxon-Protestant superiority.[32] This would influence both his interpretation and

---

31. Thomas Campbell, *Historical Documents*, 83.

32. Thomas Campbell, *Historical Documents*, 42.

formation.

Condescending attitudes, scattered throughout his publications, were often directed toward non-educated people, including the stereotypical image of Catholics. While Campbell espoused that a Christian could be identified by their transformation into the image of Christ, his expressions of disdain for differing opinions, combined with the human temptation to dominate, at times affected his formation into the image of Christ. A cursory reading of his debates denotes dogmatic stances, including derogatory remarks toward opposition.[33] Such remarks cloud his reflection of Christ. His rational and pragmatic interpretation of Scripture contributed to such dogmatic stances, yet Christ cannot be accurately reflected through a rational, scientific interpretation of Scripture.

Rational, Empirical, and Pragmatic

According to one of Campbell's biographers who had worked with him, Campbell relied on the scientific, inductive method of interpretation he learned from Francis Bacon. Using this method, Alexander sought to pull the facts from Scripture to reconstruct the primitive church and Christian system.[34] Campbell argued that the "inductive style of inquiring and reasoning is to be as rigidly carried out in reading and teaching the Bible facts and documents, as in the analysis and synthesis of physical nature."[35] This view would prove formative in his oft rigid interactions with others. He also believed that severe language was needed to "alert the church to 'the moral maladity' that consumes its spiritual life."[36] Assuming this rational method would more fully illuminate the practices of the Primitive church, the New Testament, particularly the book of Acts, became prominent for study, often to the neglect of the importance of both the Gospels and the Old Testament to the biblical narrative.

33. Douglas Foster, *A Life of Alexander Campbell* (Grand Rapids, MI: Eerdmans, 2020), 190.

34. Robert Richardson, *Memoirs of Alexander Campbell* vol 2 (Indianapolis, IN: Religious Book Service), 106.

35. Alexander Campbell, "Schools and Colleges—No. 2" MH, 3rd ser., 7 (March 1850): 172. Cited in *Declaration and Address*, 38.

36. Douglas A. Foster, Paul M. Blowers, Anthony L. Dunnavant, D. Newell Williams, *The Encyclopedia of the Stone-Campbell Movement* (Grand Rapids, MI: Eerdmans, 2004), 122.

De-Emphasis of Old Testament

In Alexander's "Sermon on the Law," he taught that since Christians were not under the law but under grace, there was no need to preach the law.[37] He concluded, "There is no necessity for preaching the law in order to prepare men for receiving the gospel."[38]

Though he recognized the patriarchal, Jewish, and Christian dispensations and believed that the New Testament could not be understood without the "history of the Jewish nation and God's government of them,"[39] over time, distinctions concerning the law would serve to disconnect the Old Testament from the New, thus neglecting a vital understanding of the story of God beginning with creation. This resulting de-emphasis of the Old Testament contributed toward what would over time become an anemic understanding of the redemptive story of God.

A redemption narrative inclusive of both the Old and New Testaments more completely informs spiritual formation, preparing one for encounters with hardship, disappointments, and defeats as they "see" God's faithfulness throughout all these dispensations and exiles. While Christians are no longer under the law, an emphasis on the New Testament without the added dimension of understanding from the Old can leave Christians ill-equipped in their formation for the deserts they will face throughout their Christian journey. The desire to restore New Testament Christianity de-emphasized the biblical narrative beginning in the Old Testament and instead focused on patterns found in the New Testament, particularly as recorded in the book of Acts when the church began to grow and spread. The focus on finding patterns through commands, examples, and necessary inferences continued, thinking this was key to creating unity.

---

37. Murch, *Christians Only*, 63-64.

38. Alexander Campbell, "Sermon on the Law," cited in Thomas H. Olbricht, "Hermeneutics in Churches of Christ," *Restoration Quarterly* 37, no. 1 (1995): 15.

39. The Christian system, https://webfiles.acu.edu/departments/Library/HR/restmov_nov11/www.mun.ca/ rels/restmov/texts/acampbell/tcs2/TCS200A.HTM.

The Pattern and Sectarianism

Seeking to defend primitive Christianity and interpretation through commands, examples, and necessary inferences found in the New Testament, the restoration ideal Campbell espoused opposed the ecumenical movement he sought. From his platform, he "launched a devastating attack on everything and everyone who did not agree with his vision of the ancient Christian faith."[40] The pattern principle, used to describe the RM hermeneutic, implies an underlying command from God which requires specific actions or attitudes along with examples of biblical characters living out these actions and attitudes, thus establishing a pattern requiring the same actions and attitudes of people today.[41]

Since Alexander Campbell considered the meaning of Bible facts to be clear, he insisted on speaking of Bible things by Bible words and called out leaders like Calvin, Arminius, and Wesley for speculative thoughts that had little to do with his perception of clear biblical facts. His rational approach to interpretation brought certainty to Campbell's views, evident in his publications and sermons.[42] Douglas Foster pens, "For him, the focus of our being in Scripture was to use our intellects to dissect it and extract the patterns of doctrine and practice we must replicate. The inevitable temptation of this understanding is that it becomes all about mastering Scripture rather than allowing God's Spirit to master us through Scripture."[43]

Unfortunately, Campbell's convictions about "the image of Christ" being the true measure of a Christian was not fully carried into the movement. Over time, followers drew tight fellowship lines.[44] Over the next century and a half, the test of orthodox Christianity for many of his followers was strict adherence to what he had formulated as the ancient gospel and order of things.

---

40. Richard T. Hughes, *Reviving the Ancient Faith*, (Abilene, TX: ACU Press and Eerdmans Publishing, 1996), 22.

41. J.D. Thomas, *We Be Brethren: A Study in Biblical Interpretation* (Whitefish, MT: Literary Licensing, LLC, 1958), 91.

42. Campbell's system of order can be seen in his publications such as the 1829 *Christian Baptist* and his theological treatise, *The Christian System*, written in 1839.

43. Richard T. Hughes, *Reviving the Ancient Faith*, (Abilene, TX: ACU Press and Eerdmans Publishing, 1996), 22.

44. Alexander Campbell, "Replication No. II to Spencer Clack," *Christian Baptist* 5.2 (3 September 1827) 370.

And, according to historian Douglas Foster, "that is exactly what Campbell had always insisted."[45] It appears that Campbell vacillated in such insistence as he also wrote that the ancient order is not a condition of Christian fellowship.[46] Though the movement began with the intent to unite all Christians through careful interpretation of Scripture, many Restoration Movement leaders showed judgmental, controlling postures, far from Jesus' attitude reflected in His example and teaching of humility (Mt 18:1-4; 23:11-12; Jn 13:12-17).

Seeing the need for spiritual formation in the church, he expressed that his movement needed fewer converts and baptisms and more nurture of converts it already had and that he sought "fewer controversies and greater efforts toward edification."[47] His writings, however, lack focus on personal spiritual, heart-felt life. His focus on Scripture was about restoring patterns, structure, and theological systems. As David Pocta notes concerning Campbell, "The idea of the Bible being a source of living water or the bread of life for the believer does not seem to fit into Campbell's imagination ."[48]

Though he later became more ecumenical, his followers did not. As Restoration leaders' patternistic interpretive methods became dogmatic, competitive, judgmental, and aggressive, converts waned, controversies increased, and disunity replaced edification. The legalistic nature of patternism had already taken root and would continue to impact future RM leaders' spiritual formation, resulting in sectarian postures.

Sectarianism: Christlike or unloving?

David Lipscomb, a third-generation Restoration Movement leader, opposed Campbell's change stating, "Many persons break away from sterile orthodoxy in their youth, but when the

45. Foster, *Life of Alexander*, 316-17.

46. Alexander Campbell, "Replication No. II to Spencer Clack," *Christian Baptist* 5.2 (3 September 1827): 370. https://webfiles.acu.edu/departments/Library/HR/restmov_nov11/www.mun.ca/rels/restmov/texts/acampbell/tcb/TCB502.HTM#Essay5.

47. Campbell, "Preface," Millennial Harbinger, n.s., 3 (January 1839): 3. Cited in Hughes, Reviving, 39.

48. David Pocta, "Thomas Wayne "Kip" McKean: Saint or Scoundrel," *Teleios: A Journal for Holistic Christian Spirituality* vol. 1, no. 2 (2012): 56.

conservatism of age comes upon them, turn back to their early faith and undo much of the reformatory work of their vigorous manhood.[49] He lauded a "hardline" stance as spiritually strong, despite the un-Christlike treatment of others that often ensued. Though Lipscomb was known as a good, loving man who sounded a call for unity, he also held tightly to patternism as he summed:

> We have no creed, no discipline, no confession of faith, no church manual, no ritual, except the Bible, the book of God Divine. We have no leader, no head, except the immaculate Child of Mary. We claim to be nothing under the shining realm except Christians—Christians only. We stand pledged to the idea of speaking where the Bible speaks and keeping silent where God's book is silent. This gives the only possible basis for Christian unity, and for its accomplishment, under the blood-stained banner of Prince Immanuel, our earnest prayers are constantly ascending toward the throne of God.[50]

He uses various examples such as Nadab and Abihu's use of unauthorized fire in Leviticus 10 and Saul's failure to completely destroy the Amalekites to lay groundwork to show God's seriousness about precision obedience as he warns of the dangers of his brethren who have allowed instrumental music to be used in their worship services. His response exemplifies the disunity that patternism can cause:

> I regret more than I can ever express to you the fact that after this movement of restoration had shaken this entire earth and made men sit up and take notice of the very fine principle, every plank of the platform of which was based upon a "Thus saith the Lord," by and by a very lamentable occurrence transpired, and that was the introduction into the service and worship of a thing untaught in the New Testament Scriptures. In the year 1869, in the city of St. Louis, there was injected into the church an instrument of music. The result was a division in what had been a happy, contented, united brotherhood. Its influence spread throughout the land, and about twenty-five or thirty years ago it struck our own beloved Tennessee.[51]

49. David Lipscomb "Tolbert Fanning's Teaching and Influence," in James Scobey, *Franklin College and Its Influences* (1906; reprint, Nashville: Gospel Advocate, 1954), 10, cited in *Reviving the Ancient Path*, Richard Hughes, 41.

50. N.B. Hardeman, *Hardeman's Tabernacle Sermons, Vol 1* (Nashville: Gospel Advocate, 1922), 86.

51. Hardeman, *Tabernacle*, 267.

Perhaps the love of Jesus that transformed the Apostle John from a young disciple who desired to call down fire from heaven on those who opposed them (Luke 9:54) into a man known in his later years as the Apostle of love could have informed Lipscomb that Campbell had chosen a more excellent way of love as he aged (1 Cor 12:31-13:3). Some other leaders were known for a more gentle and humble approach, such as a key leader, Barton Stone.

Grace and Uncertainty in Formation

Barton Stone, known as a pietist, emphasized holiness as the means to unity more than Campbell's rational, blueprint approach. Their shared commitment to restore primitive Christianity paired them as cofounders of the Restoration Movement. Both contended that Christian union could come by a return to the Bible alone as a rule of faith and practice—a restoration of the New Testament church in doctrine, ordinances, and life.[52] Stone, like Campbell, believed that Scripture was plain and accessible and that doctrines not explicitly taught in the New Testament contradicted biblical teaching and could not be true.[53]

While Stone practiced patternism, he valued spiritual experience. He espoused that some who interpreted the Scriptures in ways he thought inaccurate were more Christian than those who shared his interpretation of primitive Christianity yet engaged in sectarian, demeaning practices. Baptism was a dividing issue, and though he taught believer's immersion, he favored fellowship with Christian churches on an equal basis between the immersed and unimmersed, making Christian character the sole test of fellowship.[54] His posture demonstrated a humility of uncertainty, which led to more Christlike character and increased unity.

Effects of certainty/uncertainty and experience on formation

Stone believed that the basis of unity could never be built on speculative or controversial subjects and valued Christian experience. He admitted his own weakness when speaking of

---

52. Murch, *Christians Only*, 95.

53. Foster, *Life of Alexander*, 232.

54. Murch, *Christians Only*, 119.

theological speculation as he shared "I never preached a sermon of that kind [speculative theological discussions] that once feasted my heart; I always felt a barrenness of soul afterwards."[55] While these discussions left Stone feeling empty, such discussions often fueled Alexander Campbell's rhetoric. Did Stone's spiritual forming inform his humility and distaste for speculative arguments, or did his lack of certainty in theological interpretation feed his formation? While one may not know for sure, whenever an interpretive methodology becomes unmoving and draws deep lines in the sand, the sinful desire to dominate can take over, as demonstrated continually since the fall of humankind in the book of Genesis (Gen 3:16) to current practices. In contrast to drawing boundary lines, Stone's humility and emphasis on Christian experience reflected a more Christ-like posture than is observable from the writings of many contemporaries.

Experience informs formation

Stone's autobiography shows his belief in the importance of firsthand Christian experience. He believed it possible for the Holy Spirit to enlighten and guide one in the study of the Word of God apart from the traditional creeds of Christendom. In contrast, Campbell wrote to the editor of the *Baptist Interpreter*, "... how the Spirit operates in the Word, through the Word, by the Word, or with the Word, I do not affirm. I only oppose the idea that anyone is changed in heart or renewed in the spirit of his mind by the Spirit without the Word." [56] This clarifies Campbell's view that the Scriptures contained the Holy Spirit, and without the Word, the Spirit was not operative in one's life. This view restricts spiritual formation outside of the covers of a Bible.

Those working for recovery of primitive Christianity from Campbell's influence would become known as the churches of Christ and those more inclined toward unity of all Christians would become known as Disciples of Christ.[57] The two groups eventual-

---

55. Murch, *Christians Only*, 112.

56. Murch, *Christians Only*, 117.

57. The "c" in "church of Christ" was intentionally not capitalized to emphasize the "non-denominational" status important to the Movement.

ly separated over the issues of instrumental music in worship and the establishment of missionary societies (both were accepted in the Disciples of Christ) and in 1906 were noted in the Bureau of the Census as two distinct groups.[58] The churches of Christ would more carefully practice ecclesial perfectionism, which resulted in negative formational tendencies and greater disunity.

Ecclesial Perfectionism and Formation

As the Restoration Movement's publications began focusing more on ecclesial perfectionism, judgmental, condemning postures increased. There were a few exceptions, who practiced greater humility in their desire to imitate Christ, but most, such as early 1800s RM leader Moses Lard, practiced ecclesial perfectionism. He warned that any change of "apostolic practice' is dangerous and disloyal."[59] His publication, entitled *The Quarterly*, exemplifies many of the cynical, sarcastic attitudes evident from patternistic interpretation:

> Let us agree to commune with the sprinkled sects among us, and soon we shall come to recognize them as Christians. Let us agree to recognize them as Christians, and immersion, with its deep significance, is buried in the grave of our folly. Then in one whit will we be better than the others? Let us countenance political charlatans as preachers, and we at once become corrupt as the loathsome nest on which Beecher sets to hatch the things he calls Christians... Let us agree to admit organs, and soon churches will become gay worldly things, literal Noah's arks, full of clean and unclean beasts. To all this let us yet add, by the way of dessert, and as a sort of spice to the dish, a few volumes of inner light speculations, and a cargo or two of reverend dandies dubbed pastors, and we may congratulate ourselves on having completed the trip in a wonderfully short time. We can now take rooms in Rome, and chuckle over the fact that we are as orthodox as the rankest heretic in the land.[60]

---

58. Douglas Foster, "What Really Happened in 1906: A Trek Through History Reveals the Role of Census," *The Christian Chronicle: An International Newspaper for Churches of Christ* (April 1), 2006. https://christianchronicle.org/what-really-happened-in-1906-a-trek-through-history-reveals-role-of-census/

59. Murch, *Christians Only*, 159.

60. Moses Lard, *Lard's Quarterly*, cited in Murch, Christians Only, 159.

These biting characterizations of those who had different views of what Lard saw clearly as a biblical pattern continued with other leaders' postures toward ecclesial perfectionism. Walter Scott deserves mention as another significant preacher in Restoration History. During one of Scott's meetings, Presbyterian William Amend, who had come to similar conclusions as Scott about baptism, had a response similar to Peter's hearers in Acts 2:36-38, who were eager to be baptized right away. Scott often referred to this date, Nov 18, 1827, as the time when the ordinance of Christian baptism was for the first time in modern history received in perfect accordance with apostolic teaching and practice.[61] This bold claim hints at a common theme among many Restoration leaders to have instituted the "perfect" return to primitive Christianity. Later, wars of words in preaching and editorials would showcase a desire to be "right," "first," or "more enlightened" than others.

Scott taught a "five finger exercise" representing "Faith, repentance, baptism, remission of sins, and the gift of the Holy Spirit."[62] While I believe these elements to be scripturally true and necessary, when taught as a system of one-dimensional obedience to a pattern, the heart of Jesus gets easily lost, thus reaffirming Jesus' warning that one can miss the point of the Scriptures by pouring over the Scriptures (John 5:39). In contrast, leaders such as Isaac Errett demonstrated spiritual formation born from humility.

Contrasting views

In 1866, another influencer, Isaac Errett, began a new journal he named *The Standard*. Holding to Restoration principles outlined in his publication,[63] he was viewed as wise, compassionate, and visionary, contrasting other more aggressive, name-calling leaders. Many regarded those who disagreed with their opinions

---

61. Murch, *Christians Only*, 101.

62. Murch, *Christians Only*, 103.

63. Isaac Errett's Restoration principles were recorded in his pamphlet, "Our Position," published in 1870. Prepared by Jim McMillan in 1995 for inclusion in the RM Library of electronic texts. http://articles.ochristian.com/article15449.shtml.

not just as erring brothers, but as enemies of the truth.[64] Errett's response to such adversarial behavior denotes such a vital aspect of interpretation and formation that it merits inclusion:

Division and its roots come as readily to attempt to forbid that which Christ has not forbidden, as through an attempt to impose that which Christ has not imposed...Two things, it strikes us, must be kept carefully in mind. 1) The necessity for free and unembarrassed research with a view to grow in grace and knowledge. It is fatal to assume that we have certainly learned all the Bible teaches. This has been the silly and baneful conceit of all that have gone before us. Shall we repeat the folly, and superinduce a necessity for another people to be raised up to sound a new battle-cry of reformation? Must every man be branded with heresy or apostasy whose ripe investigations lead him out of our ruts? Must free investigation be smothered by a timid conversation or a presumptuous bigotry, that takes alarm at every step for progress? Grant that errors may sometimes be thrust upon us. Free and kind discussion will correct them...Murderous stifling of free thoughts and free speech...not only renders union worthless by the sacrifice of liberty, but will defeat its own purpose and compel, in time, new revolutionary movements. 2) The absence of all right to control our brethren where Christ has left them free. Such freedom may sometimes alarm us. Creedbound communities may lift their hands in holy horror at the "latitudinarianism" that we allow. But it is not worthwhile to accept principles unless we are willing to follow them to their legitimate results; and we insist that Romans xiv allows a very large liberty which we have no right to trench on except with the plea of the demands of Christian love.[65]

His leadership and hermeneutic moved many toward a more Christlike manner of formation. After the Civil War, the Restoration Movement numbered about 200,000, and by 1875, this number had doubled, though the growth was short-lived.[66] As leaders espoused controlling, unyielding stands on interpretation, church membership, particularly in the churches of Christ, began to decline. Professor John Mark Hicks, describing effects of patternism expounds, "Surely Alexander Campbell is turning

64. Murch, *Christians Only*, 167.
65. Isaac Errett, *The Standard*, citied in Murch, *Christians Only*, 171.
66. Murch, *Christians Only*, 214, 218.

over in his grave by now. The hermeneutic which enabled him to return to the 'ancient order' for the 'happiness and usefulness' of Christians came to serve an ecclesial perfectionism, identify the terms of communion, and practice an ecclesiology without grace."[67]

Errett's humble and uniting posture accompanied by his curious, grace-filled approach to interpreting Scripture, contrasted the control and pursuit of power accompanying leaders who pursued ecclesial perfectionism stemming from patternism. His irenic spirit spread through his publications. Moore, in his eulogy of Errett remembered, "he did much to deliver the Restoration Movement from the atavism and despotism of reactionary forces; he gave the brotherhood a high view of Christian union; and he projected a nobler conception of the task of the church and the responsibilities it imposed."[68] This trend would not last, as the twentieth century brought new challenges to formation and unity.

Twentieth Century Interpretive Trends in the Restoration Movement

For the Restoration Movement, the twentieth century began with healthier formation and a great period of church growth. Unfortunately, this would be short lived as interpretation resulted in deeper divisions and quests for power, control, and the desire to be first, right, and best. These quests would hinder formation into Christlikeness. The century began with a brighter reflection of formation into Christlikeness.

In 1909, a large centennial convention gathered in Pittsburgh. The leader-stated goals were for attendees to leave with a desire for daily worship at home, to win another person to Christ, to subscribe to two Christian papers, to give at least a tithe, to give financially to a Christian college, and to keep saloons away. They also had congregational and institutional goals such as ministry cooperation, men's organization in each church, two million dollars toward missions, benevolence, education, a thousand re-

---

67. John Mark Hicks, "Stone-Campbell Hermeneutics V-Moral and Positive Law," https://johnmarkhicks.com/2008/05/31/stone-campbell-hermeneutics-v-moral-and-positive-law/

68. Murch, *Christians Only*, 178.

cruits to ministry, two hundred thousand trained workers, and promotion of Christian union. The convention was seen as a great success, garnering the attention of the religious world. They desired to "tell the story of the Restoration Movement, give the principles of the plea, and voice a message of Christian unity."[69]

The euphoria from the conference became short lived as the RM experienced fifty years of conflict and division, particularly among the churches of Christ where patternism was most practiced. Critics targeted mission societies and the perceived commercializing of institutions as finances were raised. Others felt leaders demonstrated arrogance and pretense. The conflicts were not about the Scriptures, but rather the interpretation of the Campbell's unity methodology.[70] Arguments arose, and personalities began to oppose one another as the churches divided over issues such as Sunday schools, study guides, using more than one cup in communion, the role of women, and instrumental music. As arguments arose over interpretation, formation into the image of Christ took a back seat. Correct interpretation of a pattern was seen as the goal, rather than seeing Jesus as the pattern and the goal.

Losing the heart of Jesus in interpretation

Patternism promotes legalism which misses the trajectory of Jesus' Kingdom teachings. One could partake of the Lord's supper on the first day of the week (according to the pattern, examples, and inferences) by faith (Rom 10:17; 2 Cor 5:7), but would be sinning to commemorate his death on any other day of the week "by faith."[71] Historian and theologian Thomas Olbricht noted that for Campbell and Scott, though they taught that Christ died for the church and is its lawgiver, "then Christ is relegated backstage and the church moves up front center. Neither Campbell nor Scott concerned themselves much with the word and work of the earthly Jesus."[72]

---

69. Murch, *Christians Only*, 209.

70. Murch, *Christians Only*, 215.

71. Edward C. Wharton, *The Church of Christ: A Presentation of the Distinctive Nature and Identity of the New Testament Church* (West Monroe, LA: Howard Book House), 120.

72. Thomas H. Olbricht, "Hermeneutics in Churches of Christ," *Restoration Quarterly 37 no 1* (1995): 19.

Journals contained complicated diagrams seeking to explain "necessary inferences" such as the importance of using one cup or many during communion, prohibition of the use of musical instruments during worship assemblies, whether churches could work together to support orphan homes or missionaries, and the permissibility of kitchens in the church building. Surely, the heart of mission and caring for orphans got lost amongst diagrams and condescending arguments from leaders impugning sinful motives by those who opposed them. Patternism resisted formation into the heart of Jesus and sharing of His concerns. Numerous arguments stemmed concerning what was scripturally required and what was optional for Christians resulting in legalism, judgmental "holier than thou" postures, and fear-based allegiance, missing the heart of Jesus.

The prideful path flowing from patternism can be illustrated through a sampling of conclusions set forth in a speech during a Florida College[73] lectureship and in several widely distributed books among the churches of Christ.

- We speak of the churches of Christ in one county, in congregational sense. One church. "This should be enough to convince the most incredulous that Christ is the founder of only one church. This being true, we have no choice in the matter and should be content to be members of Christ's church."[74]

- The church of Christ is scriptural in name. The Bible condemns human names (1 Cor 1:12, 13) The name Lutheran is a human name. Therefore, "Lutheran" is under condemnation.[75] (The author uses this same reasoning to condemn all other denominations because of their names.)

---

73. Florida College was known as a conservative college run by the "non-institutional" Church of Christ.

74. Roy E. Codgill, "Biblical Authority: Its Meaning and Application," *Florida College Annual Lectures* (Marion, IN: Codgill Foundation Publications, 1974), 27. https://www.restorationlibrary.org/library/WBF/WBF_SIPDF.pdf.

75. Codgill, "Biblical Authority," 34.

- We do not use reverend, Pastor, and Father. "The church of Christ is scriptural in name and language. No man can deny it. It is the belief and practice of the church of Christ to call "Bible things by Bible names." Paul exhorted Timothy to do this saying, "Hold the pattern of sound words"[76] (2 Tim 1:13)

- The Lord's church is a New Testament institution, and the New Testament tells us of the items of worship the Lord put in it. It is evident that those who have it (instrumental music) in the worship do so without scriptural authority.[77] If men bring instrumental music into the worship today on the ground that it is mentioned in the Old Testament, consistency demands that they bring animal sacrifices and the burning of incense also.[78]

- Paul taught home is to be the center of social activity, not the church (1 Cor 11:20-22). Thus, fellowship banquets, refreshments, [and social activities] are sectarian and lead directly to what Paul condemned in Corinthians. "It is not the business of the church to provide recreational activity, thus things like rooms for ping pong or basketball leagues are a perversion of the energies and resources of the church."[79]

When such subjective methods are employed, division is the inevitable result. Jesus' strong words to the Pharisees apply, "They strain out a gnat but swallow a camel" (Mt 23:34). Such "tightrope walking" adherence to a pattern brings into view a graceless God, standing ready to punish when precise orders (often differently interpreted) are not precisely followed. When one views God and the Scriptures in this manner, harsh treatment of others follows, as demonstrated in many editorial wars and quests for power.

---

76. Leroy Brownlow, *Why I am a Member of the Church of Christ* (Ft. Worth, TX: Brownlow Corp, 1945, 57th printing 2008), 37.

77. Brownlow, *Why I am a Member of the Church of Christ*, 176-179.

78. Roy E. Codgill, "Biblical Authority," 182.

79. Roy E. Codgill, *Walking by Faith, 10th Ed.* (Bowling Green, KY: Guardian of Truth Foundation), 1984, 12.

The quest for power and its effect on formation

Churches of Christ, Disciples of Christ, and Christian churches avoided organizational structure outside of the biblical pattern of elders, deacons, and evangelists. They were, in a sense, "ruled" by publications. W.T. Moore, a preacher and editor of *The Christian Quarterly* wrote in 1809 that "the Disciples of Christ do not have bishops, they have editors."[80] Though the pattern interpretation led to a void of formalized power structure beyond the local congregation, the absence of this structure allowed leaders' oversized egos to seek power and seize control through subscriptions.

In his accounts of issue-driven conflicts, historian Richard Hughes concludes, "One cannot fully understand the battle over institutions [one of the contested principles] unless one appreciates the lust for power and control that often drives contestants in struggles such as this."[81] Preacher and writer J.D. Thomas observed that some churches were so divided over cooperation versus autonomy concerning the care of orphans, use of church buildings, and the relation of churches and schools that they [opposing forces] are willing to "burn down the house in order to kill the mouse."[82] He condemned the prevalent slander and lack of love. "We in the church preach Christian unity stronger and 'louder' than almost anyone, and surely if we but stop and think, we will all be willing to give up any personal pride and any pet peeves, so that unity can truly become a reality among the Lord's people..."[83] It became clear that unity would take more than "stopping and thinking." It would require one to be spiritually formed into the image of Christ, replacing personal pride with selfless love. Sadly, this did not often happen as demonstrated by the leadership of Foy Wallace, Jr.

Interpretation, power, and control

In the 1940s, Foy Wallace, Jr. sought to purge the church of

---

80. William Thomas Moore, *Comprehensive History of Disciples of Christ* (NY: Fleming H Revell, 1909), 12 as cited in Richard T. Hughes, *Reviving the Ancient Faith* (Abilene, TX: ACU Press and Eerdmans Publishing, 1996), 10.

81. Richard T. Hughes, *Reviving the Ancient Faith*, 228.

82. J.D. Thomas, *We Be Brethren* (Abilene, TX: Biblical Research Press), 1958, 4.

83. Thomas, *Brethren*, 5.

premillennialism and pacifism through his editorship of *The Gospel Guardian.* He gained a large following and "emerged as the single most influential preacher in the churches of Christ, with the power to crush most who resisted his opinions and leadership." [84] "Power" and "crushing" denote destructive formational tendencies for many leaders devoted to patternism. The relationship of interpretation and spiritual formation begs questions which many leaders answered poorly: Does one's view of their interpretation as *the* correct view often lead them into an aggressive, condescending, and dominating posture? Will one's stand for truth result in their desire to receive credit for a movement?

Campbell announced that the movement he led was the first in all of Christendom seeking to unite and build upon the Bible alone as he penned, "The era of Restoration will as far transcend... [the era of Reformation]...as the New Testament transcends...the dogmas...of Westminster and the canons of the Assembly's Digest." [85] His desire for "first" and his posture of preeminence over Reformation leaders further connect the relationship between one's view of their superior interpretation method and spiritual formation. This view of hermeneutical superiority not only influenced leaders' teachings and doctrines but also their personal life choices.

Contrasts: Interpretation Informs Personal Choices

Leaders' interpretations of Scripture affected their spiritual formation. [86] While Campbell should be commended for his good beginning, his rise in influence negatively affected his spirituality when he reacted harshly to those who opposed him. Stone's convictions, however, caused him to emancipate all his slaves, teach pacifism, and abstain from politics. [87] Though Campbell

---

84. Hughes, *Reviving*, 160-61.

85. Alexander Campbell, *The Christian System*, 5th Ed. (1835; reprint, Cincinnati: Standard Publishing, 1901), p. ix "Christendom in Its Dotage: A Hint to Reformers," *Millennial Harbinger* 5 (August 1834): 374; "A Restoration of the Ancient Order of Things, No. 1," *Christian Baptist* 2 (7 February 1825): 134-36; and "Prefatory Remarks," MH 1 (4 January 1830): 8. Cited in Hughes, *Reviving*, 23.

86. Spiritual formation is not meant to describe spiritual disciplines, but to describe the transformation of character into Christlikeness.

87. Hughes, *Reviving*, 108.

eventually freed his slaves, he became pro-slavery. Hughes suggests this was to save his movement.[88] While his motives can't be proved, it appears that on this issue his movement became more important than righteousness.[89] In a detailed argument drawn from biblical examples used to uphold the legitimacy of owning humans for life, Campbell sarcastically accused those who opposed slavery of creating a biblical text to justify their agenda. "'All men are born equal, comes not from Scripture but from 'Saint Voltaire,' and baptized by Thomas Jefferson.'"[90] He did not see slavery as a moral evil,[91] because of his literal view of the instructions concerning slaves in Ephesians 5, along with his "need to maintain the support of a national constituency for the success of the reform."[92] Patternism influenced formation, increasing ways to marginalize, divide, and devour one another.

While biographers note Alexander Campbell's argumentative demeanor, in contrast, his wife, Selena, wrote of her husband:

> He was always happy, cheerful; ever uncomplaining, unmurmuring, and never fault finding, always ready to find something to praise and approve of—whether at home or abroad. Such was the tenor of his noble life! Indeed how could he be otherwise than happy—love was the supreme topic with him—love to 'God supremely, and love and good will to men!'[93]

While his noble heart could be seen, history shows the tendency to lose Christlike attitudes when seeking to uphold a pattern, or a movement based on a pattern that becomes dogmatic.

In contrast, Barton Stone's view of Scripture seemed to form

---

88. In an email text on July 29, 2023, John Mark Hicks shared his belief that Campbell wanted slavery to end gradually without dividing the country and the church. However, his patternism prevented him from making a theological argument about abolition because Scripture regulated slavery rather than ending it.

89. Hughes. *Reviving,* 274.

90. Alexander Campbell, "Slavery and the Fugitive Slave Law–No. II," *Millennial Harbinger* (May 1851), cited in Foster, 285.

91. Campbell would have viewed slavery more as a political evil.

92. Foster, *Life of Alexander,* 288.

93. Donald M. Kinder, *Capturing Head and Heart: The Lives of Early Popular Stone-Campbell Movement Leaders* (Abilene, TX: Leafwood, 2012), Kindle, 52.

him differently. He lived a simple life, refusing a salary from the church. He freed his slaves and visited former slaves with prayers and affectionate tears.[94] He noted the effect of the debating spirit, warning, "debates tend to strife, deaden piety, destroy the spirit of prayer, puff up the vain mind."[95] He believed that as the size of heads increased, hearts definitely diminished. Near the end of his life, he lamented his own people placing biblical knowledge, religious controversy, and debate over "godliness, piety and brotherly love."[96] He poignantly asked: "Do we see genuine Christianity promoted by such controversies and debates? Look around and enquire for these fruits. Do you know of any person spiritually renewed or refreshed with spiritual understanding? Do you find brotherly love and Christian union advanced? On the contrary, do you not find their opposites promoted?"[97] Stone noticed that when the Scriptures were read, the expounders sought to establish their received doctrines of controversy more than humbly seeking His will. He warned, "When the pulpit is ascended, the burden of the sermon is the agitated controversies of the day, teaching the congregation the art of war."[98] According to Stone, within a generation, attention and energy began to be focused on maintaining true doctrine.

John Rogers, one of Stone's biographers, who was also a preacher in the Stone-Campbell Movement, said this of Stone:

[His] entire life has been made of tenderness, amiability and love. As a husband he was fond, indulgent, kind. As a father, he was mild, affectionate, impartial. As a brother, faithful; as a friend, ardent and unwavering... The cause of his Savior was nearest his heart, in youth, manhood, and old age. Christianity was his theme in life—his comfort in death.[99]

94. Kinder, *Capturing Head and Heart*, 47.

95. Kinder, *Capturing Head and Heart*, 78.

96. Kinder, Capturing Head and Heart, 81.

97. Kinder, *Capturing Head and Heart*, 32.

98. Kinder, *Capturing Head and Heart*, 28.

99. Rogers' biography of Stone quoted in Mathes, *Works of Elder BW Stone*, and cited in Kinder, 73. Also see chapter IV, https://webfiles.acu.edu/departments/Library/HR/restmov_nov11/www.mun.ca/rels/restmov/texts/jmathes/webws/WEBWS04.HTM

Stone's humility could be seen in his words, writings, and deeds. In the introduction to both editions of his *Address* he wrote:

> Believing mankind to be fallible creatures, we therefore feel a spirit of toleration and union for all those Christians, who maintain the divinity of the Bible, and walk humbly in all the commandments and ordinances of the Lord Jesus Christ, and who live by faith in his name, though they may hold opinions contrary to ours.[100]

Contrasts in the formational tendencies of leaders varied. Some leaders' insistence on adherence to certain patterns often influenced a lack of grace or judgmental postures leading to arrogant postures while the hermeneutic and posture of others, like Stone, encouraged formation leading to humility and grace.

Conclusion

The Restoration Movement's desire for unity and reverence for Scripture remain noble passions reflecting God's heart as expressed through the life and teachings of Jesus. Restoration leaders, attempting to restore primitive Christianity, viewed Scripture through a lens of patternism, looking for commands, examples, and necessary inferences. Often, their desire for ecclesial perfectionism resulted in legalism, disunity, arrogance, control, and condescending postures, thus dimming the reflection of Christ in their lives. When the leaders believed they had mastered Scripture drawing from the pattern they interpreted, they drew sharp boundaries, placing the Bible in a proverbial box. Their interpretation method often showcased a desire to master a blueprint, rather than be mastered and transformed by the author of the blueprint, the Living Word.

The tendencies toward being first and best, gate keepers, and ecclesial perfectionists will remain as long as interpreters search for the patterns they deem to be commands, examples, and necessary inferences. This certainly does not mean truth is relative.

---

100. Barton Stone, "An Address to the Christian Churches in Kentucky, Tennessee, and Ohio on Several Important Doctrines of Religion, 2nd Edition," (1821), https://webfiles.acu.edu/departments/Library/HR/restmov_nov11/www.mun.ca/rels/restmov/texts/bstone/ADDR-2ND.HTM

However, patternism takes certain first-century, often-occasional teachings and dogmatically sets them in stone. It defines negotiable and non-negotiable interpretations, often neglecting the first and greatest command to love the Lord with all one's heart, mind, soul, and strength and one's neighbor as themselves (Mt. 22:37-39). As Jesus stated, all the law and prophets hang on these commands.

History repeatedly practices large pendulum swings of reaction and overreaction. Generations react to the beliefs of the previous generation. In the later nineteenth century, as frontier revivals erupted, those fearful of the emotional responses desired a religion more tamed and certain. Campbell's model had spawned a dominance of reason over experience or emotion, journals, and debates.[101] Donald Kinder notes that "by the twentieth century, fewer and fewer actively thought about the place of the heart. This oversight was by no means intentional, but the belief was there that if the head were aligned properly one need not worry much about the heart. It would surely follow. The only problem was that it did not."[102]

Historical practices grow deep roots not easily altered. The hermeneutic of the RM historical leaders still lingers, and the resulting judgmental, legalistic postures continue to affect the formation of Christians in RM churches, often in unsuspecting ways. To turn this tide, greater awareness and teaching of both history and hermeneutics become necessary. Otherwise, we will not recognize the waters in which we swim.

---

101. Kinder, *Capturing Head and Heart*, 81.

102. Kinder, *Capturing Head and Heart*, 180.

103. Illustration by Moxin Qian, based on a parable by David Foster Wallace that illustrates how people cannot recognize the influence of their surroundings while immersed in them.

CHAPTER TWO

The Pattern Persists: Current Views Using Old Prescriptions

Not everything that is faced can be changed.
But nothing can be changed until it is faced.[104]

Writings from early Restoration Movement leaders depict ways their hermeneutics affected their spiritual formation. Their pleas for unity, born from adherence to biblical patterns, quickly morphed into judgmental, pharisaical postures resulting in conflicts and divisions. Though some RM churches have revised their pattern hermeneutic, this method of interpretation formed deep roots that continue to inform spiritual formation. Such inveterate thinking and behaviors continue among her members, thus adjustments to the current hermeneutical lens will require a thoughtful, intentional process, discerning its virtues and vices.

Hermeneutical lenses require re-examinations to determine whether they are adequate for spiritual formation or if they need further adjustments. Christlike transformation, or lack thereof, in both individuals and spiritual communities serve as indicators of healthy or unhealthy lenses. Jesus, in His concern for the poor taught the importance of the lenses we use: "Your eye is the lamp of your body. When your eyes are good, your whole body is full of light. But when they are bad, your whole body is full of darkness."[105] Hermeneutical lenses that distort the *imago Dei* have far-reaching effects, as seen throughout RM history, and even now in the International Churches of Christ (ICOC), the RM branch where I am a member.

During its brief history, the ICOC has undergone several adjustments in interpretation, born more from pragmatism than

---

104. James Baldwin, "As Much Truth as One Can Bear," an essay printed in the NY Times on January 14, 1962.

105. In Luke 11:34, Jesus addressed ways Pharisees misinterpreted God's laws.

clear hermeneutical adjustments. After an international church-wide "firestorm"[106] early in the twenty-first century, my church needs a lens re-examination to evaluate the strengths, weaknesses, and relevancy of its current hermeneutic. Prayerfully, this re-examination can help clarify and reframe blurred, problematic views of interpretation, encourage greater depth in spiritual formation, bring greater reliance on the Spirit of God, and find unity that often eludes our grasp.

A Hermeneutical Crossroads

Currently, the ICOC stands at a hermeneutical crossroads. Though once-argued issues in the RM, such as the use of instrumental music in worship and participation in missional cooperation are non-issues in the ICOC, other issues take their place. The ICOC has often employed, likely without realizing it, an adjusted form of patternism. Intentional teaching about our RM history and our hermeneutical lens rarely, if ever, takes place in our churches, and there are currently few attempts to explore or reframe our hermeneutic. This void in teaching creates confusion concerning ways some scriptures are interpreted and taught. Consequently, this affects unity in and among the churches, particularly concerning disputable matters such as the role of women in the church. For some, such issues are disputable. Others see these same issues as clearly defined by a biblical pattern meant to be continually followed.

Other issues with differing interpretations include divorce and remarriage, elders and believing children, the role of evangelists, the importance of one church-one city, pacifism, house churches, and baptismal cognizance. Church life practices among members can quickly move from good practices to church rules. With good intentions to help young couples maintain purity in their relationship, challenges arise when these intentions become rules rather than convictions based on heart-felt desires to please God and treat one another with love and purity. Also, baptism might be delayed for someone who has not completed all the stud-

---

106. Author Ron Susek termed an ignited church conflict a "firestorm" in his book, *Firestorm: Preventing and Overcoming Church Conflicts* (Ada, MI: Baker Books, 1999), 13.

ies in our Bible study series, despite the urgency of the one desiring baptism. Rule-based practices such as these often hold their roots in the pattern hermeneutic. Though ironically, there are no dating practices or study series for baptismal readiness in the New Testament, set and expected practices are often espoused to uphold the teachings of the Bible, and can soon become rules of the church rather than issues of one's heart. Members, over time, can be left with shortcuts for well-intended practices without understanding the heart of God and the ways that one's heart transforms their desires. Though "issues" are discussed, the hermeneutics from which differing opinions arise often remain undiscussed. Biblical scholar N.T. Wright observed, "The Bible seems designed to challenge and provoke each generation to do its fresh business, to struggle and wrestle with the text."[107] With this in mind, I believe the church has "fresh business" to do. Its history includes strengths and weaknesses of interpretation and wrestlings with the text.

The Birth of the Boston Church of Christ and the ICOC

During the 1960s, several churches of Christ were influenced by a reform movement for campus ministries. The largest and most influential campus ministry, where hundreds of college students were converted, took place at the University of Florida, in Gainesville. This group was not so focused on following a pattern, but on calling each new convert to serious discipleship, something often absent in the churches of Christ during that time. Among the converts was Thomas Wayne "Kip" McKean.

In 1979, a fledgling church of Christ in Lexington, Massachusetts, invited McKean to lead the dying church. Kip had been converted as a University of Florida college student in the nearby and vibrant Crossroads Church of Christ campus ministry.[108] After graduating and serving full-time in campus ministry in Illinois, he eagerly answered the call to move to Boston because of his desire to work with its high impact campuses. He had long been a fan of Harvard University. The Lexington church of Christ had been in the Boston area for years, but had few members when

---

107. N. T. Wright, *Surprised by Scripture* (NY: Harper Collins, 2014), 29.
108. It would appear that Crossroads missed the memo concerning the lower case "c," as they capitalized "Church."

McKean arrived. It grew quickly and dramatically, and in 1983 became known as the Boston Church of Christ. The church took the
great commission seriously and began planting churches around
the world, beginning in London a year earlier, in 1982. This group
would eventually become 700 churches in 147 nations.[109]

In the late 1980s, many young leaders who had been part of
the mainstream churches of Christ moved to Boston to join her
mission to evangelize the nations. The Boston Church of Christ
saw great growth in its first decade and a half, so much so that
Time Magazine featured the controversial church in an article.[110]
In 1993, the Boston church and her plantings became known as
The International Churches of Christ, a name given to the group
by researcher John Vaughn in his publication *Church Growth Today*. The mainstream churches of Christ had previously removed
the Boston Movement churches from their church listings, due
to faults they perceived in the ICOC.[111] The Boston Movement
also wanted distinction from the mainstream churches of Christ,
which they saw as uncommitted to whole-hearted discipleship.

Thomas A. (Tom) Jones, who served as an elder in the Boston
church and editor of its publishing arm notes: "Burned by some
attempts to work within existing churches, Boston had decided to
be a completely separate movement without connection to others.
At best, this was a mistake. At worst, it was a sin. In either case,
it led to a form of sectarianism, and this is now clearly seen by
many who remained with the movement."[112] With that fear, Jones
also expressed that there was another concern that "increased
connections with those in other fellowships may lead us back to
that comfortable Christianity that is so at odds with the Jesus of the
New Testament."[113] This intersection requires prayerful navigation.

109. Charles Wayne McKean, "From Jerusalem to Rome, from Boston to Moscow: Revolution through Restoration
1," http://www.usd21.org/wp-content/uploads/2012/06/Revolution_Through_Restoration.pdf, 7. Cited in
Douglas Foster, "The Stone Campbell Movement and the International Churches of Christ," *Teleios Journal*, vol.
1, no 2 (2021): 36.

110. Richard N. Ostling, "Keepers of the Flock," *Time Magazine*, May 18, 1992.

111. John Vaughn conversation with Roger Lamb, former editor of "Disciples Today." Tom Jones remembers the
removal from church listings from an article in the "Christian Chronicle."

112. Thomas A. Jones, *In Search of a City: An Autobiographical Perspective on a Remarkable but Controversial
Movement* (Spring Hill, TN: DPI, 2007), 91.

By 1990, McKean had moved to Los Angeles and the center of the movement shifted from Boston to Los Angeles. By 1995, the Los Angeles ICOC was the fastest growing church in the United States, and churches of over 1,000 members were meeting in each of these cities: Tokyo, Moscow, London, Johannesburg, Mexico City, Hong Kong, and many others.[114] The ICOC quickly became the fastest growing church in the RM and trained thousands of leaders, but in the late 1990s the growth leveled off due to a high percentage of people leaving the church. Since its beginning, the ICOC has grown to a current worldwide membership of approximately 100,000,[115] but overall the church has lost 72% of the new members.[116] Certainly, this lack of retention should cause introspection concerning spiritual formation. Patternism does not deserve credit for all the strengths or blame for all the weaknesses in the ICOC, but I believe at its root, it brings both significant contributions and problems to spiritual formation.

The ICOC's brief history, its relationship to a pattern interpretation of scripture used in the RM, and the resulting spiritual formation of its leaders and members remain a work in progress. The ICOC churches were unique among the RM churches in their call for a renewed focus and plan for missions, a decisive call to wholehearted discipleship (termed "total commitment" during the Crossroads campus ministry era),[117] racial diversity, care for the poor, and the expectation of involvement in one another's lives.[118] To better understand a correlation between the ways the pattern hermeneutic still affects us, it seems important to observe strengths and weaknesses of this interpretive method.

---

113. Jones, *In Search of a City*, 94.

114. "Progress of World Evangelism." *KNN* Episode 7.

115. This membership was reported in 2019 by Douglas Foster, "The Stone Campbell Movement and the International Churches of Christ," *Teleios Journal*, vol. 1, no 2 (2021): 36. At its peak, the ICOC church membership was close to 140,000.

116. Andrew C. Fleming, "Let Each One Be Careful How He Builds: A Study of the Statistical Narrative of the International Churches of Christ," *missionstory.com* (April 2018). https://www.archive.missionstory.com/ICOC_Culture_and_Narrative_Articles/let-each-one-be-careful-how-he-builds-(2018).html.

117. Many of the influential ICOC church leaders had been converted through a vibrant campus ministry at the Crossroads Church of Christ in Gainesville, Florida in the 1970s.

118. Douglas Foster, "The Stone Campbell Movement and the International Churches of Christ," *Teleios Journal*, vol. 1, no 2 (2021): 36-38.

Patternism's Strengths

Any hermeneutical lens has both strengths and limitations. Though patternism, when used as a singular hermeneutic has many flaws, there are important and needed aspects to this interpretive method which help to ground and grow a Christian. The RM's focus on the Bible and its high view of Scripture result in most members being biblically literate. In the ICOC, members are encouraged to read the Bible every day, read it with their families, memorize scriptures, and use scriptures in their conversations with each other. The church teaches the importance of obedience to God and to the Scriptures. These are great strengths within the church.

Patternism encourages imitation (of biblical patterns), which greatly aids new converts coming out of destructive, sinful lifestyles. Patterns, in this way, encourage spiritual formation with their simplicity and specific direction. Patternism helps keep members tethered to Scripture, which helps strengthen and form them. David Pocta recounts strengths of patternism after he was converted from a worldly lifestyle:

> I needed a radical break from the bad behaviors I had developed, and stepping into a world where I was called to imitate and put into practice things I not only saw in the Bible but saw in Christians around me transformed me. It was wonderful and needed, and my conversion was radical. I have zero regrets. Teens and campus students need patterns to follow to learn disciplines like prayer, fellowship, showing up at church, and discipling times.[119] It gives a necessary ethos to build the container right, but once the container is built, we get stuck in self-help, not knowing how to move deeper.[120]

Patternism's strengths bring order to Christians, until the patterns become problematic. Pocta, comparing many aspects of patternism to fundamentalists, shared an insight from his mentor, Ronald Rolheiser: "Fundamentalism isn't necessarily wrong, it's just extremely anemic."[121] Pocta believes it to be a great foundation for laying a core foundation with imitatable qualities:

---

119. Discipling times were times set between two Christians to look at Scriptures, pray, confess, and discuss their spiritual lives.

120. David Pocta Zoom interview, October 20, 2022.

121. Pocta quoting a conversation with Ronald Rolheiser during Zoom interview, October 20, 2022.

It's brilliant at the early stages of formation as a young Christian laying foundations, such as those taught in Acts 2:42: "They devoted themselves to the apostles' teaching and to the fellowship, to the breaking of bread, and to prayer."
Over time, patternism comes up empty, because it doesn't have life beyond that
imitation. Patternism is all about imitation.[122]

Though some RM churches, including the ICOC, have adjusted some old lenses of patternism, those lenses still have deep
roots employing old prescriptions.[123] Despite many strengths,[124]
the legalistic and often judgmental lenses of patternism remain incomplete, anemic, and problematic for spiritual formation, as can
be seen by the divisions among early RM leaders and subsequent
judgmental, divisive postures among RM churches. The old pattern prescription fails to fulfill, sustain, unify, allow room for the
Spirit, and focus on the heart of Jesus. It is clouded by a focus on
the blueprints intended to restore New Testament patterns, often
missing the big picture the blueprints should produce.[125] Patternism can be nuanced, at times taking on more pragmatic qualities.

Patternism and Pragmatism

Tom Jones, in his historical memoir, *In Search of a City*,
notes that our [ICOC] primary approach in interpretation is
pragmatism.[126] Pocta observes that our interpretation started as
patternism and shifted to pragmatism.[127] McKean wanted to get
the job done to accomplish his vision, which was the driving force
that shaped many dec.isions.[128] From these pragmatic decisions,
patterns were often tacked on as prooftexts, finding justification
from the Bible to indicate that we were still following the pattern.

---

122. David Pocta interview.

123. Some of the issues of patternism were discussed in chapter one, including issues such as using instruments in worship, Sunday school, church kitchen, mission societies, societies helping orphans, and one cup for communion. These issues came from an intent to follow commands, examples, or necessary inferences seen in the New Testament.

124. A strength of patternism is that it is a form of imitation, nuanced by context and theology.

125. Jesus referred to the weightier matters as justice, the love of God, mercy, and faithfulness (Lk 11:42, Mt. 23:23).

126. Jones, *In Search of a City*, 106, 108.

127. In an email July 29, John Mark Hicks noted that patternism cannot address all the pragmatic questions that disciples have in seeking to follow Jesus. Thus, patternism reverts to pragmatism to address urgent questions.

128. David Pocta interview.

McKean used, found, and employed biblical patterns in new ways, usually applying them to help accomplish his vision for the church. These included his view of a blueprint from first-century churches for one church in a town. This pattern supported his "one church, one city" teaching. If more than one church existed in a city, it erred from the biblical pattern. He envisioned "pillar churches" in the largest cities, patterned after the churches in Antioch and Ephesus,[129] and to make them strong he often took both full-time and lay leaders from smaller churches, calling them to move to the "pillar churches."[130] Many church leaderships were ravaged, while the churches were still held accountable for strong growth. Since the pillar churches covered expansive geographical areas, one could question whether the pillar churches were built to follow a biblical pattern, as taught, or if they were built to be the "biggest and best" for less honorable reasons. McKean also used Colossians 1:23 as a pattern. Here, Paul shared news that the gospel had been preached to the whole world, which for McKean supported the "biblical pattern" of reaching the entire world in one generation. He taught, "Some have questioned whether it is God's command to go to 'every nation in a generation.' Literally in the Greek text of Matthew 28, Jesus commanded the eleven apostles to 'disciple and then baptize all nations.'"[131] This became the pattern to be followed in this generation. To accomplish this, he came up with a six-year-plan of church plantings that far exceeded the church's readiness or maturity to accomplish.

Pocta would argue that the ICOC's downfall began with the creation of the "Six-Year Plan."[132] The battle to maintain that document and its goals became unhealthy, ending with a fight for the institution more than Jesus. One wonders if many were converted to a movement or to a method of discipleship more than to Jesus, given the number who left.

During his Boston ministry tenure, McKean adjusted the

129. Historic Christianity called such "pillar" churches as Pentarchy: Rome, Constantinople, Alexandria, Antioch, and Jerusalem. They were Patriarchates of the church.

130. As recorded in the Boston Church of Christ bulletin, January 4, 1987.

131. Kip McKean, "From Babylon to Zion: Revolution Through Restoration III," http://www.usd21.org/wp-content/uploads/2012/06/Revolution_Through_Restoration.pdf (accessed November 14, 2022), 7.

132. David Pocta interview.

ICOC hermeneutic from the RM mantra "speak where the Bible speaks and be silent where the Bible is silent" to "be silent where the Bible speaks and speak where the Bible is silent."[133] However, like the earlier version of patternism based on commands, examples, and necessary inferences, confusion and disagreement arose concerning when and where the Bible truly spoke and when and where it was silent. In 1993, McKean developed a lesson on "wine, women, and song" for the churches, changing the previous practice of abstinence from alcohol to allowing the use of alcohol (without drunkenness). The new teachings also allowed women to part-sing in front of the church, serve communion, share alongside a man at a communion testimony, and baptize other women. A cappella-only singing, which was the practice in public worship, changed to allow for the use of musical instruments. While McKean adjusted the hermeneutic on these "issues," his interpretive methods still leaned heavily on patterns.

Concerning the ICOC use of pattern, Pocta adds:

> We would use the book of Acts to justify why we were the movement of God, because we believed the pattern was that that wherever the Spirit was, the church grew. Therefore, because we were growing, the Spirit was clearly there. Thus, if you are not in a church that is growing, you are not part of the Spirit's movement. Patternism works when it works, until it doesn't work. Then everything gets shuffled, and an identity crisis ensues.[134]

The use of such a pattern fit well with McKean's focus on growth. Jones suggests that his pragmatic hermeneutic was likely not a conscious hermeneutical teaching.[135] The ensuing misuse of Scripture led to various doctrinal stands that became important in the movement.

Though some might argue that the ICOC no longer uses a pattern interpretive method, some of her practices and resulting spiritual formation/deformation suggest otherwise. Patterns can be

---

133. McKean, "From Jerusalem to Rome," http://www.usd21.org/wp-content/uploads/2012/06/Revolution_Through_Restoration.pdf (accessed November 14, 2022).

134. David Pocta interview.

135. Jones, *In Search of a City*, 107.

used for all sorts of practices and can tempt one to prooftext rather than understand the intended meanings within the scripture. The ensuing misuse of Scripture led to various doctrinal stands that became important in the ICOC, and even today McKean's pragmatic hermeneutic affects our teaching and forming. Tom Jones cautions, "as we collect our practical wisdom, we must not 'absolutize' it or elevate it to the level of eternal truth."[136] Doing so can demonstrate one of patternism's weaknesses.

Patternism's Vices

Though there are strengths in patterns, especially for young Christians, serious problems can trace their roots to a pattern mindset. These include pharisaism, as seen in the Gospels, neglect of a Jesus-focus, self-help over Spirit-dependence, gnat-straining and dissection, sectarianism, arrogance, formulizing God's heart into a function (seeking to master Scripture), certainty over humility, a lack of curiosity to learn, and pragmatic proof-texting. In exploring these vices, I recount RM leadership historical accounts, historical data of church divisions, judgmental postures exhibited in RM journals and writings, ICOC history, and interviews from members often unknowingly influenced by and reacting to these vices.

Pharisaic legalism

At its core, patternism breeds legalism. Author Shari Simpson-Cabelin, a former lay leader in the ICOC, shared her thoughts on problems that arise when one puts the Bible in a box, then pulls it out of that box to find a pattern and state the rules:

> JESUS is the Word of God. The Bible is a story that, like the treasure hidden in a field, requires work, discernment, and clear-eyed recognition of what sort of book it is. And it is not a law book, a rule book, a yardstick, a monolith, a cudgel to beat people into submission, a way for people to stay in power over others, a management tool, an iron gate that keeps the people out we disagree with, a pattern that we have to figure out and get just right because if we don't, we get

---

136. Jones, *In Search of a City*, 46.

sent to hell. The Bible is not univocal, it is multivocal, meaning that it has multiple voices that combine into a messy, limited view of a limitless God, not a neat, systematic package that God dropped down to Earth fully formed. It does not lend itself to certainty, which we love, but faith, which is uncomfortable... The Pharisees held the scriptures in a tight fist; when they were asked to open their hands in generosity, they found themselves unable to do so. Jesus stood before a group that wished to condemn him for healing on the Sabbath because "the Bible says so"—he looked past/through the words on the page to the suffering of the man in front of him and did the work of God, not the directives of a rule book written in stone.[137]

These words describe the ease of movement from patternism to pharisaical legalism, and the resulting thoughts and behaviors so displeasing to God.

Jesus spoke harshly to the Pharisees who came after Him for distorting God's truth by adding to it. He rebuked them for straining out the gnats and swallowing camels.[138] His desire for justice, mercy, and faithfulness (relational issues) was overtaken by these Pharisees' gnat-straining issues.

Though history shows Alexander Campbell vacillating between humility and dogmatism, if his words on Pharisaic postures in the RM were indeed heeded, interpretation would not lead to sectarianism:

Dear sir, this plan of our own nest, and fluttering over our own brood; of building our own tent, and of confining all goodness and grace to our noble selves and the elect few who are like us, is the quintessence of sublimated phariseeism. The old Pharisees were but babes in comparison to the modern, and the longer I live, and the more I reflect upon God and man, heaven and earth, the Bible and the world, the Redeemer and his Church, the more I am assured that all sectarianism is the offspring of hell...To lock ourselves up in the bandbox of our own little circle; to associate with a few units, tens or hundreds, as the pure church, as the elect, is real Protestant monkery, it is evangelical phariseeism.[139]

---

137. Shari Simpson-Cabelin written interview, Nov 3, 2022.

138. Mt 23:23-24.

139. Alexander Campbell, "Letters to an Independent Baptist," *Christian Baptist*, Vol 3, No 10 (May 1, 1826), https://webfiles.acu.edu/departments/Library/HR/restmov_nov11/www.mun.ca/rels/restmov/texts/acampbell/tcb/TCB310.HTM

The added rules from patternism can put more focus on issues than on Jesus, resulting in attitudes that look down on others who don't share the same views, and thus missing the heart of Jesus. The first-century church was not the first-century church simply because they were trying to create a pattern to follow. Instead, they were trying to be like Jesus.

A blurred view of Jesus

Many, if not most of our church members, read the Bible with an underlying pattern hermeneutic resulting in a common mantra, "The Bible said *it*, I believe *it*, and that settles *it*."[140] Leaders and teachers can contribute to this by thinking they have or should have the answers to "it." A hermeneutic focusing on an "it" which stems from the heart of God displayed in Jesus, rather than oft-disputed patterns, will lead to deeper spiritual formation resulting in greater unity.

Jesus taught that people, particularly leaders, can pore over the Scriptures, yet fail to see them pointing to Him (Jn 5:39). Patternism encourages comfort of consistency with a practiced pattern, yet the pattern can often become more of a focus than the reason for the pattern. After one healing touch, the blind man, as recorded in Mark 8:24, saw people, but they looked like trees. He needed another touch from Jesus to see clearly. Patternism promotes a blurred view of Jesus, turning Scripture into biblical patterns. Patternism needs a second touch from Jesus, clarifying the view of that which He values most.[141]

With patternism's desire to imitate the New Testament church, the book of Acts naturally became the dominant book for Bible study.[142] Since Jesus' ministry took place during the time when the Old Covenant was still in effect, and the RM sought to become the New Testament church, the study of Acts has often taken precedence over Jesus' teachings about the Kingdom

---

140. This phrase was made popular after used by Ernest Angley in an article he wrote in December, 1998 entitled, "God said it; I believe it, and that settles it!" https://www.ernestangley.org/read/article/god_said_it_i_believe_it_and_that_settles_it (accessed May 17, 2023).

141. Mt 22:36-40.

142. ICOC ministers were trained to teach classes on First Principles and the book of Acts.

of God.[143] Because Acts historically (in the formative years of the ICOC) garnered more attention than the Gospels, it follows that formation centered more on church growth and practice than heart teachings on qualities Jesus most values. The teaching and practice of discipleship, often lacking in other churches, has been known as a great strength in the ICOC.[144] Yet, the function of doing in discipleship can overshadow the who disciples are to follow. When a pattern takes precedence over the heart behind that pattern, dogmatism surely follows.

Dogmatic Postures

Teacher Steve Staten describes the relationship between patternism and our church culture, noting that Scripture is made of narratives, and some interpretations are guesses when we do not really know the contexts. And we cannot fully know the contexts. Patternism takes guesswork out of interpretation. Even though the interpreters do not really know the context, they bind the surface understanding.[145] Staten continues:

> We had our own patterns and people promoting unique patterns different from the patterns of the mainstream (church of Christ). More often, they were centered around hierarchy, centralized leadership, and evangelists over elders. There was one template, largely borrowed from the early church in Ephesus, and that was the way we were to 'do' church.[146]

The ICOC went through many of its younger, formative years using a hierarchical practice of "discipling."[147] While there is great value in an older Christian mentoring a younger Christian, patternism encouraged young leaders and evangelist-focused

---

143. Tom Jones, ICOC teacher and former publisher of DPI, the ICOC's book publisher for many years, shared these thoughts in an interview on 10/26/22. Because of this lacking in the ICOC teaching, he has authored three books about the Kingdom of God.

144. ICOC movement has often been defined as a "discipling movement."

145. Steve Staten Zoom interview, October 11, 2022.

146. Steve Staten interview.

147. Discipling is the term commonly used in the ICOC for relationships to help each other grow.

churches to decide what the pattern (or inferences) of Christian behavior should be. Advice, especially on disputable matters, often became dogma. This led to subjective interpretations of scriptures concerning church practices that too quickly became dogmatic. Though this culture has changed significantly in many places, the wrong ways it was practiced were not widely addressed as wrong teachings, and the wrong teaching was certainly not communally lamented.

There were "actions" such as sharing one's faith with strangers that were seen as necessary aspects of readiness for one's baptism. Outward means for maintaining purity, often helpful to young Christians, often became dogmatic, such as the practice-become-rule for double dating only and various other dating practices that often were communicated through one's discipleship partner. Financial giving required accountability and at times, people were strongly discouraged from moving to another state that would take them away from their current church location, even when the financial strain for their family felt unbearable in an expensive part of the country. When the heart of Jesus was neglected in the attempt to restore New Testament Christianity, practices became human-made rules. The examples used show the formation of rules while seeking to follow a biblical blueprint. The obvious irony would include the lack of practices of dating, job related moves in the New Testament church, weekly church collections, and myriad other practices for which the Bible has no pattern. Though some of these rule-based practices have changed in many of our churches, many still remain, and the undergirding history and hermeneutic remains unknown to members. The ways these were taught in many of the older member's formative young Christian years can often serve as their default ways of thinking.

When heart issues become formulas

In the late 1990s and early 2000s, the church leadership measured success by church attendance and growth. The leaders with the fastest growing churches were praised and highlighted at conferences. Small group leaders (most often lay leaders), during their weekly leaders' meetings, were responsible for recording and publicizing their group's church attendance by members and visitors, the number of visitors at their small group Bible studies, the collection amount, and whether each person had given what they had pledged to give. Leaders were taught to measure whether they should feel "good, great, or awesome" by the number of visitors that each "feeling" represented. Though not part of the RM churches, Author Tim Soerens describes such a phenomenon: "We blunt and minimize the potential power of the local church by turning it into a commodity purchased with our attendance at an event."[148] While these deforming practices (based on the pattern assumption of church growth as the main indicator of the Spirit's approval) are no longer employed, their use in many Christians early and formative stages of growth affect their formation today.[149]

In more recent years and in response, some of the larger churches have instituted excellent teaching programs, taking members deeper into their Bible knowledge and applications and teachings on grace, the Spirit, and formation. While some things have been done to address the needs, many churches still offer little more than First Principles classes,[150] Sunday sermons, and perhaps midweek classes or sermons that are often pragmatic in nature. There remains a need for teaching and training in church history, and an adjusted hermeneutic that tends to spiritual formation from the inside out. Many members are hungry for such, as can be noted from the thousands of participants in recent grass-roots-led Spiritual Formation seminars and workshops.[151]

---

148. Tim Soerens, *Everywhere You Look: Discovering the Church Right Where You Are* (Downers Grove, IL: Intervarsity Press), 2020, 17.

149. Growth was carefully measured with accountability during the late 80s and the decade of the 90s in the ICOC. The high accountability is no longer practiced in most churches, but years of intense focus on growth and high accountability taught a way of formation centered on numerical growth.

150. "First Principles" was a class developed by Kip McKean and taught to members on how to study the Bible with others. The topics of seeking God, the Bible as the Word of God, sin, repentance, baptism, and the church were taught in this class. While it was incomplete, it equipped Christians, young and old, to help someone become a Christians through the vehicle of this Bible study.

151. Tim Soerens, *Everywhere You Look: Discovering the Church Right Where You Are* (Downers Grove, IL: Intervarsity Press), 2020, 17.

These offerings explore the "heart" of the Scriptures more than the rational patterns, a crucial exploration for all Christians, especially those questioning and deconstructing their church beliefs and roots.

Observations from the trenches concerning patternistic formulas and dogma

Since many of our youth are "deconstructing" their faith, and prayerfully trying to reconstruct it, I shall use a representative of their voices, as told in a recently published book by a young man who grew up in the ICOC and served as a youth leader in his teen and campus years. He expresses his thoughts on spiritually deforming effects that ICOC "patterns" had on his and his friends' lives. While his story does not attempt to reflect everyone's experience, his story reflects the experiences of far too many, particularly those who grew up in the church.

His chapters express "truths" he learned in the ICOC vs. truths he believes are more aligned with God's ways. Concerning the teaching on conversion, Austin Noll writes:

> When I was growing up, there was a process that one was required to go through if they desired to get baptized in our church. They would need to be led through a series of curated Bible studies, where they would be taught the fundamentals of Christianity and Jesus. For what they provided, these studies did an adequate job of teaching us the information necessary to decide on getting baptized, while often falling short of providing the true heart and soul-level wealth that the good news offers. However, if you were in youth group, from middle to high school, you usually weren't permitted to jump straight into the "core" Bible studies. First, you had to complete what were referred to as "character studies," which were about as on the nose as they sound. Once a week, a leader would lead you through a lesson focused on one particular aspect of your character, whether it be pride, honesty, obedience, humility, etc. They weren't always the same for each kid either. They were directly contrived from whatever aspects of their character the leader deemed they most needed to improve. Basically, it was a weekly self-improvement course you were forced to go through if you wanted to become a Christian.[152]

---

152. Austin Noll, *A Jumble of Crumpled Papers: A Church Kid's Journey from Confidence, to Questioning, to Christ* (Kindle; Austin, TX: Wise Path Books, 2022) 31-32.

The pattern of the steps to become a Christian often went beyond the Scriptures, as the meanings of what it means to be "cut to the heart" or "repentance" before baptism (Acts 2:47-48) were subjective. These patterns became part of church culture still in existence today, rooted in subjective interpretations of perceived biblical patterns. Another danger in following a blueprint is the temptation to gain God's and others' acceptance through one's own efforts in following that pattern.

Patternism as Self-Help

Patternism becomes self-help when adherents seek to "function" themselves into relationship with God through following the pattern of Scripture, rather than functioning out of that relationship. By mastering Scripture in search of certainty, self-reliance subtly replaces Spirit-led formation with dogmatic postures. This difference affects spiritual formation, particularly in areas of self-reliance and/or leader reliance. It leads to the thought that overcoming sin or weakness means one must do more, following a pattern that functions them into transformation. They metaphorically row their own formation boat, rather than hoist the Spirit's sail.

Noll offers axioms of truths and untruths: More Rules = Less Room for Mistakes. He contrasts this untruth with the truth of: More Rules = Less Room for God. He views these rules as promoting the lifestyle of that which they seek to inhibit. While he shows honor and respect for God's commandments, he proposes:

> The plethora of superfluous rules that we have added and allowed to shape our lives and spiritual communities have only damaged and reinforced the notion that we aren't fully confident of our complete freedom from condemnation. And to those on the receiving end of said condemnation, who aren't assured of this truth, there is only one belief to gain: if other followers of God condemn me, then God must condemn me as well.[153]

---

153. Austin Noll, *A Jumble of Crumpled Papers: A Church Kid's Journey from Confidence, to Questioning, to Christ* (Kindle; Austin, TX: Wise Path Books, 2022) 31-32.

Noll continues, as he explores the tendency toward self-help over the Spirit's lead:

...you were not allowed to advance to the subsequent character study until you proved that you were making progress on improving whatever part of yourself you were currently focusing on. And it was never based on how you felt you were doing. It was always up to whether or not the leader believed you were ready. We literally had Jesus gate-kept from us by our own church. We started these studies because we genuinely desired to know and follow Jesus, yet we were told that we could only begin to do so once we worked on ourselves first. As if Jesus wouldn't accept us for who we were. And we believed it. We would spend weeks, months, being led through study after study working on ironing out all of our perceived character flaws while the cookie that was Jesus was being dangled right in front of us, always one step out of reach. Many kids didn't make it through these character studies and ended up backing out before they were even given a taste of what they had come for in the first place, which was Jesus. I always cringe when I remember my own studies when I was on track to getting baptized... It was a flawed system, based solely on self-improvement and outward perfection while completely ignoring the basis for why someone would want to learn about Jesus in the first place. Countless numbers of young people, many who are my friends and peers, were taught that if they wanted to follow Jesus, they would have to meet Him halfway. Sure, He could help you with your problems and make you a better person, but you would first need to fix many of your biggest problems yourself... The phrase "get right with God" is already problematic because of how incapable we are of doing that, let alone the fact that it is somehow now a task we must do to secure our salvation. Simply put, it doesn't make sense. That idea suggests that our redemption is contingent on our own ability.[154]

This self-help approach can also affect formation in leaders, creating a trap that once a leader perceives what they believe to be God's dreams or patterns on an intellectual level, then it is up to them to make it happen, or at least communicate it on a broader, bigger, and better stage. This trap tempts certainty rather than humility. Timothy Soerens speaks to this phenomenon:

---

154. Noll, *A Jumble of Crumpled Papers*, 162.

> I can easily take this world-changing hope and make it useful. I don't need God to actually be at work in people's lives. I just need a meta story so I can get it to work. I'm in charge, with a newfound theological energy that leads me to be the savior. When I have the story but don't need God to be active in it, I have way more agency and know that at the end of the day this was my work.[155]

Certainly God can even use one's misdirected motives to accomplish His will. While Noll acknowledges gratitude for countless changed lives, he also attributes an over-concern of numbers, mission, and cause with a loss of love. Just love. He asks his former church family to refrain from viewing people as projects and instead, to be viewed as souls to be loved.

The difficulty in discerning the combination of grace and truth can seem large. Both are necessary, which is another reason patterns can only go so far. The Bible is so much more than a book of doctrine. Jesus, as the perfect embodiment of grace and truth (Jn 1:14), must become the pattern. A pattern derived from subjective interpretation tempts one to try to master and control the Bible, leading one away from humility. To enhance greater growth toward Christlikeness, our hermeneutic must be re-examined and further touched by Jesus. If the blind man needed a second touch from Jesus to see clearly, perhaps we still need that second touch in re-examining the lens through which we view Scripture. The lens through which we read and interpret should bring continual transformation into the image of Christ (2 Cor 3:18) and must be framed with humility. Unfortunately, the quest for power often clouds the lens of humility.

Patternism and Power

As a result of the influence of power over humility, conflict between ICOC leaders and members grew. This friction resulted in a church-wide disceptation at the turn of the century, and the church was forced to redefine its values, discerning the good from the bad. McKean was at the helm of church leadership

---

155. Tim Soerens, *Everywhere You Look*, 41.

during this time, and similar to some earlier leaders in RM history, it was important to McKean that he was credited as leader of the movement. His document, "Revolution through Restoration," and a website promoting his history and vision for the church showcased his belief in his role as the God-appointed leader of the movement.[156] He included in the ICOC "First Principles" follow up study series specific dates to be memorized by all members, including the beginning of "God's modern-day movement," which he attributed to "thirty would-be disciples" in a living room in Concord, MA, in 1979. All members were to take this class, which included memorization of the date of the "first second-generation disciple," the date when his oldest child was baptized. Later, after he was removed from his position of leadership, he left the ICOC and formed another group, beginning his own school of missions and a new "Sold Out Movement." He gave his leaders new and bigger titles and awarded himself, his wife, and a few other leaders doctorates, which would not be recognized in academia (outside of the state of California), but fed his desire for "first and best."

Jack Reese comments on the tendency of people to look for these types of leaders in distinct situations, particularly in times of difficulty noting, "In such difficult times, people often look for commanding leaders, sometimes autocrats or even despots, who see the world in black and white. These sorts of leaders provide unambiguous answers in uncertain times. They soften people's fears by slaying the people's enemies, whether real or imagined."[157]

Patternism's focus on being right has often invited pride, greed, and control, which takes one away from formation into Christlikeness. Walter Brueggemann writes:

> The church exists to embrace the desire of God. That embrace is not a task to be performed by our best effort and commitment, but we are invited to notice what God's own Spirit is doing in the world, nothing less than 'deconstructing and obstructing our contemporary towers' of pride, greed, and control.[158]

---

156. David Pocta, "Charles Wayne McKean," 47.

157. Jack Reese, *The Blue Hole* (Grand Rapids, MI: Eerdmans, 2021), Kindle, 117.

158. Walter Brueggemann from the Foreword of Tim Soerens, *Everywhere You Look*.

His sentiments would have been helpful to the ICOC leadership, as the leader's vision became equated with the desire of God. Total commitment, a good and necessary response to the love of Christ, became overly centered on human effort, and as a result pride, greed, and control would become issues in the church. These issues would rise to the forefront of relevance as the ICOC entered the twenty-first century.

The powder keg and the match

The desire to dominate has raised its ugly head since the fall of humankind, as recorded in Genesis 3:16. This desire to dominate does not need patternism to exist, but the pattern hermeneutic combined with a desire to dominate became toxic within the RM and the ICOC, serving as fodder for fire. When one tries to prove their position to be "the most right," as did some early Restoration leaders, the temptation for pride and control often follows, negatively affecting spiritual formation.

When RM leaders allowed patternism to mix with their pride, explosive and disunifying results followed. In contrast, other RM leaders stood out as spiritual formers, rather than judgmental deformers. Likewise, our recent history showcased leaders who foddered the fires of disunity, contrasted by other leaders who brought spiritual health to situations where embers lay ready to ignite. Unfortunately, because the movement leader, Kip McKean, led from a position of authority and power, others followed suit. While the human condition of pride sparked the fire, patternism provided tinder and kindling. Kip had set patterns of growth taken from Acts and set a specific pattern of discipleship as the proof of spirituality and the presence of the Holy Spirit.[159] Many of his patterns became deeply dogmatic.

The ICOC leadership model resembled the Catholic leadership model. In *The First Jesuits,* John O'Malley notes that "the pope had the broad vision required for the most effective deployment in the vineyard of the Lord."[160] Likewise, it was

---

159. Interview on Zoom with Douglas Jacoby, October 18, 2022.

160. Cited by James Martin, *The Jesuit Guide to (Almost) Everything: A Spirituality for Real Life* (San Francisco: Harper One, 2012), 270.

assumed that McKean had the broad vision for the most effective deployment of missions. A talented visionary, he certainly assumed this, as did others. Patternism does not necessarily lead to power abuses, nor does one's power necessitate reliance on patternism. However, when the two combine, history shows they feed each other. When this happens, spiritual formation stalls, and becomes deformation. A firestorm that had been brewing in the ICOC would become a counter-movement of sorts. Soerens describes undercurrents that brew before movements begin: "Right before most movements, the following almost always occur: People are afraid to vocalize big, important questions; polarization and a sense of nostalgia escalate; and disconnected grassroots experiments take place on the margins.[161] He concludes that "movements happen when people who thought they were alone discover they are not."[162] Certainly, these undercurrents were stirring, and members in the trenches realized they were not alone.

Firestorm 2003

Throughout the Bible, God uses surprising ways to bring change. Change may involve marching around cities and blowing trumpets or hearing a still, small voice.[163] In 2003, the ICOC experienced a firestorm that brought changes to the ICOC. Author Ron Susek defines a firestorm as an ignited church conflict.[164] The firestorm seemed sudden, but it had been brewing for years. The firestorm ignited in February 2003, when church leader Henry Kriete wrote a letter to a few ICOC leaders that was broadcast on the internet. His letter was not the cause of the firestorm, just the spark that lit the tinder.

Kriete wrote of deforming practices he saw in the ICOC leadership including a corrupted hierarchy, shameful arrogance, obsession with numbers, and seduction by money. These result-

---

161. Soerens, *Everywhere You Look*, 7.

162. Soerens, *Everywhere You Look*, 13.

163. Joshua 6:1-27; 1 Kings 19:11-13.

164. Ron Susek, *Firestorm: Preventing and Overcoming Church Conflicts* (Grand Rapids, MI: Baker Publishing, 2007), 13.

ed in heavy-handed treatment of others, favoritism, entitlement, fear-producing control, and transferring leaders from smaller churches to strengthen pillar churches leading to toxic church situations.[165] The issues were not concerning the old patterns like using one communion cup or many mini-cups, Sunday School, or instrumental music, but were rooted in some of the unfortunate ways biblical practices were interpreted and used for certain dogmatic church practices.

In her book, *Redeeming Power*, Diane Langberg explains:

> Abusive power violates and shatters relationship. It brings betrayal, fear, humiliation, loss of dignity, and shame. It isolates, endangers, creates barriers, and destroys bonds. It destroys empathy, trashes safety, and severs connection. Abusive power has a profound impact on our relationship with God and others. Victims of abuse view God through a gravely distorted lens, seeing him as the source of the evil they experience. The violation and destruction of faith at times of tremendous suffering is one of the greatest tragedies of the abuse of power.[166]

The ICOC paid a price for abuses of power. While the ICOC firestorm led to a dark time resulting in a dramatic decline in membership, full-time staff, and people's idealism, many churches entered times of healing. Some churches found healing more difficult than others. Many leaders expressed humble, public repentance, but some did not. While many leaders had not participated in abusive practices, those practices had been allowed to continue, even if leaders did not know how to stop the cycle. Many in the ICOC concluded that God intervened, creating a healthier, humbler fellowship, albeit still unknowingly rooted in patternistic interpretation.

Discerning the good and bad

It feels like a difficult task to focus on church problems while holding great admiration and respect for my church. I can list countless wonderful things in my church tradition, and it remains my family. There are many groups across our fellowship where

---

165. Henry Kriete, "Honest to God" Revolution through Repentance and freedom in Christ, DouglasJacoby.com: Articles, 2 (Feb, 2003) [online]; accessed 11 Feb 2013; available from http:// douglasjacoby.com/articles/1511-honest-to-god-by-henry-kriete.

166. Diane Langberg, *Redeeming Power* Kindle edition (Ada, MI: Baker Publishing, 2020), 7.

love for God and others shine brightly. Throughout the churches one can find large groups of campus students, teens, and adults of all ages who hold a deep love and passion for God, help each other, show up for each other, sacrifice their time and money, love the Bible, love their communities, serve the poor, and hold a passion to take Jesus to the world. Our churches are racially, ethnically, and socio-economically diverse, unlike much of Christendom today. The church shines through its service arm, HOPE *worldwide,* serving disenfranchised communities around the world. Many of the remaining church leaders lead from a desire to serve. They seek to combine a prophetic voice and shepherd's heart, not an easy task. These outstanding qualities of the church deserve praise. Yet an underlying patternistic interpretation of Scripture can tempt us to keep God boxed within patterns, inhibiting a more experiential relationship with God and restricting unity with others outside the ICOC tribe.

Many are eager to grow beyond a one-dimensional view of Christianity. They desire a unity beyond their own tribe.[167] The excellent attributes I listed are some of the "baby" that needs to survive and grow as the deforming bathwater from patternism's negative characteristics is emptied. The ability to distinguish the forming and deforming effects of patternism remains crucial for achieving an enhanced relationship with God and greater unity with others. The strengths, weaknesses, limitations, and blind spots in patternism must be taught to be overcome. Discernment of the strengths and weaknesses can prayerfully usher in increased openness to an adjusted hermeneutic, thus opening doors to greater formation and unity which have been God's desire since the beginning of humankind.

Conclusion: The Humility to Examine

Soon after He created humankind, God confronted a people out of control. They needed rules and patterns to become a civilization, a people. They learned from the priests, teachers, and

---

167. This statement is in response to the spiritual forming groups overwhelming attendance and the growth of grass roots social media groups like "Common Grounds."

prophets of the Old Testament. When Jesus came, he taught the *whys* of the rules and the goal of the fulfillment of rules living in the upside-down Kingdom of God. The pattern hermeneutic, deeply engrained in the RM and the ICOC, focuses on the *what* more than the *who* and *why*. This view encouraged a legalistic interpretation throughout the Restoration Movement's history, and is still far too prevalent. Though the patterns employed in the ICOC tended toward the pragmatic, they still created a tendency toward uniformity more than unity. The Restoration Movement's desired goal to restore the patterns of New Testament Christianity not only often missed the occasional aspects of the Epistles and varied ways to interpret scriptures, but often neglected a focus of forming one's heart into the heart of Jesus. Jesus points us to the way of the heart through the transformative work of the Spirit, which cannot be contained within a blueprint.

Spiritual formation involves a process of learning, conforming, and transforming. The early stage of spiritual formation is like a child in preschool and kindergarten, where they learn the rules without the big picture. This is needed at the beginning of one's development, but our fellowship can stay stuck in the early stages.[168] It takes humility to see and respond to the need for something more. One will not re-examine their own presuppositions and perspectives without humility.

Patternism, especially when combined with power, becomes toxic and sadly, humility can get lost in the search for certainty. The church would do well to reexamine and readjust its hermeneutical lens to pave a clearer path toward the heart of Jesus. Vision becomes blurred in the search for *the* right patterns, the *necessary* inferences, the places where the Bible speaks, and the places it is silent. The desire to be right can breed pride and sectarianism. In contrast, humility breeds curiosity, eagerness to listen, and quickness to give another credit.

Tom Jones reminds of the path to humility: "We are all naturally prideful. We defend our way and our methods and our theology. We are reluctant to give others credit. The only hope

---

168. This thought is from a Zoom interview with Robert Carillo. October 20, 2022.

for any kind of godly unity is that we crucify our pride and learn humility from Jesus. Almost daily meditation on Ephesians 4 will be needed.[169]

> As prisoners of the Lord, then, I urge you to live a life worthy of the calling you have received. Be completely humble and gentle; be patient, bearing with one another in love. Make every effort to keep the unity of the Spirit through the bond of peace (Eph 4:1-3).

We are not meant to master the Scriptures as we seek to interpret them, but instead to be mastered by the Christ who authored them. Renewed focus on Jesus and the Spirit of God brings humility and dependence that result in transformation from the inside out.

170

---

169. Jones, *In Search of a City, 149.*

170. Saji George, https://twitter.com/S_A_J_I/status/110040087445782528

CHAPTER THREE

Adjusting the Lenses:
A Clearer Hermeneutic for
Spiritual Formation

When we are securely rooted in personal intimacy with the source of life, it will be possible to remain flexible without being relativistic, convinced without being rigid, willing to confront without being offensive, gentle and forgiving without being soft, and true witnesses without being manipulative.[171]

Thus far, I have shown that the Restoration Movement's pattern hermeneutic often contributes to judgmental, domineering, and pharisaical postures, and that this lens needs adjustments. Spiritual formation that fosters greater Christlikeness will require new prescriptions to the RM default hermeneutical lens. While I have noted numerous strengths that come from careful adherence to the pattern of Scripture, the pattern hermeneutic has proved anemic for continual spiritual growth and unity.

Jesus teaches that the greatest commandment is to love the Lord with all one's heart, soul, mind, and strength (Mt 22:36-38). This marks the highest formative goal for a Christian's life, followed by the command to love one's neighbor as themselves (Mt. 22:39). To be formed toward this love, a hermeneutic must bring one's heart, mind, soul, and strength to the reading of Scripture. The pattern hermeneutic employs the mind (knowing) and strength (doing), but falls short in encompassing one's heart and soul. How might an adjusted hermeneutic remain true to Scripture while also more fully attending to one's heart and soul?

In exploring answers to this question, I shall first identify presuppositions brought into interpretation, consider ways patternism can inhibit the Gospel message, and finally, suggest adjustments to the pattern lens through the integration of a theological,

---

171. Henri J.M. Nouwen, *In the Name of Jesus: Reflections on Christian Leadership* (New York: Crossroad Publishing, 2002), 45-46.

redemptive/trajectory, and Spirit hermeneutic. I chose these lenses because, like patternism, they value the authority of Scripture and the attention to careful exegesis, but they also fill gaps found in the pattern hermeneutic. They help complete the reading and interpretation of Scripture through lenses that assist in spiritual formation and attend to one's heart, soul, mind, and strength. While the pattern engages one's mind, a theological lens focuses on the heart and character of God, concentrating on His attributes and the big picture narrative of Scripture. The Spirit lens enlivens the soul, exploring the mysterious innerworkings of God and His presence and transformative involvement in the Christian's life. The trajectory/redemption lens offers greater depth to strength, since it shifts the focus from self-help to movement toward God's desired will. While these lenses can be employed by all evangelical churches, the RM churches' default "mind-centered" blueprint hermeneutic merits the need for teaching and consideration of additional lenses to foster healthier spiritual formation.

To suggest needed components to the RM anemic interpretive method, I shall first profile major proponents of each of these hermeneutical lenses, including the pattern lens. I shall then view a passage of scripture through these different hermeneutical lenses, showing ways each highlight different emphases which directly and indirectly affect spiritual formation. A further look into the lens of patternism through the eyes of contemporary proponent F. LaGard Smith can shed light on additional forming/deforming effects from patternism.

Is There Really a Need for More? F. LaGard Smith

Current proponents of the pattern hermeneutic, including best-selling author F. LaGard Smith, consider a call for a "new hermeneutic" the result of the world's culture influencing the church more than the church influencing culture. Smith, raised in the non-institutional conservative branch of the RM, adheres to a pattern he sees in Scripture that restricts the use of musical instruments in corporate worship and restricts women from serving in any form of leadership where men are present, even passing communion trays.

Smith argues that today's liberal lobby enforces our postmodern cultures of "new morality" (or amorality) through a mind control known as "political correctness" and fears it is strikingly similar to the call for a new hermeneutic in the church. He proposes that the "radical shift from rational thought to intuitive, experiential perception" is another indicator of the culture influencing the church. He points to the strengths and weaknesses in viewing "narrative" as a new hermeneutic, cautioning its path toward a slippery, subjective view of the Bible. He then proposes an umbrella hermeneutic of "purpose, principle, and precedent" to interpret the different genres of literature in the Bible while "retaining the commendable features of "command, example, and necessary inference."[172] This seems nothing more than a rewording of command (purpose), inference (principle), and example (precedent).

Smith annunciates his plea:

> What we need is a way of understanding the Bible that calls us higher. A hermeneutic that leads us away from Self and into the mind of God is a hermeneutic born of humility. A hermeneutic that robs us of unworthy motives and gives us a grand vision of what we could be with God's help is a hermeneutic worth fighting for. A hermeneutic which dares to be counter-culture when culture would lead us astray is a hermeneutic that can safeguard our eternal destiny when culture will have ceased to exist.[173]

His concerns that many who search for a new hermeneutic in the RM do so for the wrong reasons and are more self-serving than theological.[174] He seeks to make his point using his views concerning the role of women:

> Hardly any biblical principle is more clearly established than the principle of male leadership. It begins at Creation, with Adam being created before Eve—a preview of the responsibility for leadership which would later be thrust upon all firstborn Sons...Even in the consequences attendant upon their sin of

---

172. LaGard Smith, *The Cultural Church: Winds of change and the call for a "new hermeneutic* (Nashville, TN: 20th Century Christian, 1992), 20-21.

173. Smith, *The Cultural Church,* 31.

174. Smith, *The Cultural Church,* 82.

disobedience, Eve is told: 'Your desire will be for your husband and he will rule over you.'[175]

Smith's assumption of no other correct way to interpret these scriptures stems from his view that abdication of *clear biblical principles* such as these are indicative of self-serving postures. His subtle, or not so subtle, use of certainty for an issue widely disputed among scholars who also adhere to the authority of Scripture casts disparity on anyone who thinks differently from his views.

His main "evidence" for the call for a new hermeneutic rests most explicitly on the role of women in the church and the "clear" commands from Scripture prohibiting their leadership. His words give evidence to spiritually deforming practices that arise when relying on the pattern hermeneutic—a temptation to judge and demean one who holds a different view. While reviewing the role of women in the church he states:

> The message [on women's roles] itself is clear and unequivocal; but the message is not one we want to hear. So what are we to do? Given our cultural commitment to tolerance, utility, and political correctness, we have no other choice. In order to avoid hearing the message, we're going to have to shoot the messenger! And the messenger in this case is the "old hermeneutic." "Give us another messenger," cries the cultural church. Give us a new hermeneutic that will permit us more freedom. Give us a new hermeneutic that doesn't bind us to legalistic doctrine, inductive reasoning, scientific method, simplistic blueprints, sterile constitutions, or common sense understanding of God's Word. Give us *anything* that will affirm our commitment to cultural thinking and justify the conclusions we have already reached. If possible, of course, make it *sound* spiritual—perhaps a "hermeneutic of the cross." Dress it up in culturally acceptable terms like *justice* and *equality,* and be sure to throw in a generous heaping of biblical *love.* Make it look sufficiently respectable and maybe no one will notice that what we've really done is to abandon scriptural authority. So the messenger was killed and the cultural church roared its approval: "The old hermeneutic is dead! Long live the "new hermeneutic!"[176]

175. Smith, *The Cultural Church*, 83.
176. Smith, *The Cultural Church*, 86-87.

Smith's cynical rant mirrors journal writings and word wars by early RM leaders who impugned motives and employed sarcastic put-downs in their "defense of the Scripture," furthering my proposition that a pattern hermeneutic tempts judgmental and dogmatic postures.

Smith's words exemplify forceful and fear-producing rhetoric practiced by early RM leaders, including major proponents of unity like David Lipscomb, who warned his Christian sisters that "'women in pants' on the rostrum, or managing conventions not only disobey Paul's commands for silence but are also in danger of 'eternal death' in spite of all their 'tender, tearful, heartfelt talks.'"[177] Though Lipscomb was known for his desire for unity, the pattern hermeneutic tempts one to bring judgmental proclamations such as this, which do not help unify.

Smith assumes patriarchy as God's established and created order and does not entertain other views. He attributes attempts to "soften" God's clear order and commands as acquiescing to culture and political correctness.[178] His views of male authority are unrelenting, attributing Deborah's leadership in the Old Testament to a "rebuke aimed at the men of Israel who had reneged on their leadership responsibility."[179]

Smith shows ways church creeds have often substituted for Scripture. However, his view that the RM avoids creeds falls short. He states: "Over time, however, more attention is paid to the creed than to Scripture itself. What allows this to happen is the fact that creeds crystalize a particular interpretation of Scripture. That is precisely where our hermeneutic is different. It commits us to the authoritative leading of Scripture without stating any doctrinal beliefs."[180]

---

177. David Lipscomb, "An Unjust Charge," *Gospel Advocate* 34 (Dec 1, 1892): 756, quoted from Fred A. Bailey, "The Disciple s Path," 514 and cited in a paper by Bill Grasham, "The Role of Women in the American Restoration Movement." https://www.kwcoc.org/hp_wordpress/wp-content/uploads/2017/07/WomensRoleAmericanRestorationMvmntGrasham.pdf. Lipscomb was a proponent of unity in many of his teachings, but words such as these, based on his hermeneutical lens, create barriers toward unity in diversity.

178. Smith, *The Cultural Church,* 78.

179. Smith, *The Cultural Church,* 83.

180. Smith, *The Cultural Church,* 35.

His statement assumes that the RM pattern hermeneutic is free from crystalizing a *particular interpretation* of Scripture, yet he has crystalized a particular and unyielding interpretation of Scripture. This has historically and continually formed judgment, division, and arrogance. While Smith sees "the pattern" as a necessary model for Christian living and for corporate worship, he acknowledged that it falls short with scriptures pertaining directly to life and godliness, since life and godliness insists one looks more to a *Person* than to a *passage*.[181]

His inconsistencies show in his call to follow *the biblical pattern* for corporate worship. While he views some topics, such as a cappella singing and no women in leadership as clear biblical patterns, he does not include the culturally informed practices of foot washing, holy kisses, wearing of head coverings, abstaining from gold or braids, tongue-speaking, or raising holy hands in prayer as patterns transcending culture.

Smith has little patience for the Eastern mindset of mystery in interpreting Scripture. He expresses concern to any change from the rational approach of the pattern hermeneutic as he opines, "The more likely, and even scarier alternative is an 'anti-sense' approach to Scripture, wherein there is a subjective, mystical reading of the text. Discarding the more obvious 'common sense' reading of a passage, the subjective 'anti-sense' approach risks coming away from Scripture with nothing but 'non-sense.'"[182] Here again, his certainty disparages the intelligence and character of one who differs from his views.

Inside Voices concerning patternism

John Mark Hicks, also part of the RM family of churches, explains that patternism assumes there is an ancient order prescribed by God which is uniformly present in the New Testament. It also views contextless data as historical facts that can be linked to generate new, inferred truth that fills gaps in the "clearly defined" order in Acts and the Epistles. Then, through induction and deduction, one can find the blueprint for restoring the primitive

---

181. Smith, *The Cultural Church*, 38.

182. Smith, *The Cultural Church*, 121.

church for today.[183] Though this is no longer his hermeneutic, his explanation shows reasons adherers hold their views as certain.

Gabriel Santos, a former professor who now serves as an ICOC minister, voices his thoughts on patternism, noting that when one reads Scripture as a performance or check manual for getting to heaven, they "are not able to read Scripture poetically, cyclically, or with an appreciation for many layers of meaning in a given text or across texts...If this is our primary way of reading, where is the space, the silence, for the God of peace to speak?" [184]

Church of Christ historian and scholar Thomas Olbricht wrote his summary on a patternistic interpretation of Scripture. "I myself think that a hermeneutic must revolve about, not so much the questions we wish to put to the Scriptures, but the questions the Scriptures wish to put to us. Biblical theologians are the ones who attempt to locate these questions through identifying the central issues of the biblical faith."[185] Olbricht's summary supported the importance of being mastered by Scripture rather than mastering scriptures. He acknowledges elements of uncertainty patternism does not allow.

Voices outside of the Restoration Movement applicable to patternism

While the patternist finds comfort in certainty, theologian and author Philip Yancey, who was raised in an independent fundamentalist Baptist church, addresses the formative dangers of certainty as he pens:

> Reading church history, not to mention reflecting on my own life, is a humbling exercise indeed. In view of the mess we have made with crystal-clear commands, the unity of the church, love as a mark of Christians, racial and economic justice, the importance of personal purity, the dangers of wealth—I tremble to think what we would do if some of the ambiguous doctrines were less ambiguous.[186]

---

183. John Mark Hicks, "Searching for the Pattern," *Teleios: A Journal to Promote Holistic Christian Spirituality* vol 5, no 1 (2023): 77.

184. Gabriel Santos, PhD, "Dopamine Hits, Tweets, and Rage," *Teleios: A Journal to Promote Holistic Spirituality,* vol 3, no. 1 (2023): 42.

185. Olbricht," Hermeneutics," 34.

186. Yancey, *The Jesus I Never Knew* (Grand Rapids, MI: Zondervan, 1995), 44.

Yancey continues with observations important to formation as he writes, "Churches that leave room for mystery, that do not pretend to spell out what God himself has not spelled out, create an environment most conducive to worship. After all, we lean on God out of need, not out of surplus."[187] It is such need that helps form humility, yet the patternist's desire for certainty inhibits humility in interpretation.

Timothy Soeren continues this concern as he states: "If there is certainty, if there is no risk, if we are in charge, we can't call it faith. Once we feel like we have the answer and our job is to simply strategize and implement, we are on a slippery slope toward either pride or shame."[188] These postures of certainty can feel firm and non-yielding, but they often lead to authoritarian ways as James Poling suggests:

> Research on the relation of biblical texts to the communities that produced and interpreted them is changing the assumptions about Bible study. Rather than search for a single, true interpretation of the Bible for all times, scholars are asking what a particular text meant in a particular community and how that meaning changes as the community context changes... Discovery of the metaphorical nature of language helps us see the value and the limitations of various linguistic expressions, and it may free us from a correspondence view that can function in authoritarian ways that undermine full participation in community process.[189]

The search for a pattern, when interpreting ancient Near Eastern culture, often results in similar authoritarian function of that culture, though today domination of slavery is much less common (in America) and polygamy is illegal. Early church history, Reformation history, Restoration Movement history, as well as recent scandals in numerous churches accentuate the human desire to dominate. In fact, "domination history" begins in Genesis 4, soon after Adam and Eve are expelled from the Garden of Eden after they sinned. This fallen humanity desires to dominate, and when a hermeneutical lens espouses certainty, there is little hope for seeing every human soul on level ground, at the foot of the cross.

---

187. Yancey, *The Jesus I Never Knew*, 47.

188. Tim Soerens, *Everywhere You Look: Discovering the Church Right Where You Are* (Downers Grove, IL: IVP, 2020), 41.

189. James Poling and Donald E. Miller, *Foundations For a Practical Theology of Ministry* (Nashville, TN: Abingdon Press, 2000), 22, 25.

These tendencies merit examination as the patternist views often lead toward dogma, yet this does not mean that there can be no convictions concerning right and wrong, as Smith warns.

Relevancy of an adjusted or "new" hermeneutic

Smith's concerns do hold some merit, however, in a post-modern culture where much is deemed relative, sin is not biblically defined, and one's identity is defined in whatever way they, she, he, or it so desires. He offers a charge that must be considered in discussions concerning additional lenses for interpreting Scripture. "Todays' call for renewed spirituality will have to stand the test of true holiness."[190]

New lenses must not be used to cloud the Gospel message of salvation, but must be examined to bring into clear view that very message. Otherwise, the current lenses can distort the Gospel message of Jesus. However, patterns can distort the Gospel message of Jesus just as easily as postmodernity. Perhaps less certainty that results in dogma can bring greater clarity toward that Gospel view.

Brené Brown, known for her research and insights into human behavior, reports that today's consumers of information are most persuaded when uncertainty remains part of the equation. Perhaps this study of human nature reflects some of the problematic formation stemming from patternism:

> As consumers of information, we have a role to play in embracing a more nuanced point of view. When we're reading, listening, or watching, we can recognize complexity as a signal of credibility. We can favor content and sources that present many sides of an issue rather than just one or two. When we come across simplifying headlines, we can fight our tendency to accept binaries by asking what additional perspectives are missing between the extremes. This applies when we're the ones producing and communicating information, too. New research suggests that when journalists acknowledge the uncertainties around facts on complex issues like climate change and immigration, it doesn't undermine their readers' trust. And multiple experiments have shown that when experts express doubt, they become more persuasive. When someone knowledgeable admits uncertainty, it surprises people, and they end up paying more attention to the substance of the argument.[191]

---

190. Smith, *The Cultural Church*, 215.

191. Brené Brown, *Atlas of the Heart: Mapping Meaningful Connection and the Language of Human Experience* (NY: Random House, 2021), Kindle edition, 70-72

Brown's research would suggest that a posture of humility and uncertainty is more likely to help one see the Gospel of Jesus than the self-assured, legalistic, and judgmental postures often accompanying patternism. While elements of faith such as one Lord, one faith, one baptism, one God and Father of all (Ephesian 4:4-6) are reflected throughout Scripture as non-negotiable, perhaps a patternist's deeming of "non-negotiable" interpretation of some scriptures that are widely interpreted by biblical scholars become a great hindrance in portraying the Gospel of Christ. What one deems as negotiable versus non-negotiable is often informed by their presuppositions, and every generation and culture is steeped in them.

Presuppositions in Interpretation

Readers interpret the Bible through their views of what is important, often stemming from their presuppositions. Many of the RM leaders using a pattern hermeneutic serve(d) as lawyers.[192] It makes sense that arguments and judgements drawn from a pattern hermeneutic fit them well. Likely, each person's background, training, and personality (think Enneagram or Myers-Briggs) brings tendencies toward a particular hermeneutic. Spiritual formation often begins with self-awareness. Twentieth century RM leader K.C. Moser wisely warned, "The real student is an adventurer in search of truth. He should have no preference as to what truth is. The partisan spirit has no place in the study of truth. To permit some preconceived notion to keep one from seeing or admitting truth is beneath the dignity of the real student."[193] Even so, as Alan Jacob notes, "We cannot separate who we are as persons from how we read, understand, or reflect. Ethics (how we behave) and hermeneutics (how we interpret) are necessarily linked.[194]

192. Alan Jacobs, *The Theology of Reading: The Hermeneutics of Love* (Boulder, CO: Westview, 2001); Fritz Oehlschlaeger, *Love and Good Reasons: Postliberal Approaches to Christian Ethics and Literature* (Durham, NC: Duke Univ Press, 1993), 9-48; George Steiner, Real Presences (Chicago: Univ of Chicago Press, 1991), 155-158.

193. John Mark Hicks, "Searching For the Pattern," *Teleios: A Journal to Promote Holistic Spirituality,* Vol 5, No 1 (2023): 74.

193. From the journal of K.C. Moser, 1937, 53. Sent by historian Bobby Valentine on April 28, 2023.

194. Alan Jacobs, *The Theology of Reading: The Hermeneutics of Love* (Boulder, CO: Westview, 2001); Fritz Oehlschlaeger, *Love and Good Reasons: Postliberal Approaches to Christian Ethics and Literature* (Durham, NC: Duke Univ Press, 1993), 9-48; George Steiner, Real Presences (Chicago: Univ of Chicago Press, 1991), 155-158.

Western Christians, understandably, most often approach the Scriptures through a Western lens, a patriarchal lens, and a church tradition lens. When one adds a pattern lens to these common presupposed lenses, it evokes a sense of certainty in interpretation to the presuppositions already in place. It then becomes difficult to explore new, unfamiliar waters. Blinders to one's lenses often stem from fear. These include fears of asking questions that don't conform to long-held doctrines of church tradition, and fears to question God's sometimes seemingly perplexing actions. The fear of being wrong and the fear of change also loom large when interpreting the Bible.

Blinders to the lenses through which one views Scripture include their unique life story including family dynamics, trauma, neglect, loss, ethnicity, gender, socio-economic factors, education, political background, social systems, and religious traditions. People interpret the Bible through all these obstacles. Only when one becomes self-aware of the blind spots resulting from their presuppositions will they be open to a lens adjustment. If one thinks they already see clearly, they will see no need for adjustments. Jesus said long ago, "Though seeing they do not see; though hearing, they do not hear or understand" (Mt 13:13). Since no one is exempt from presuppositions, it can be assumed that lens adjustments will always be needed. Adjustments to the pattern lens needed to encourage a more Christlike formation will require new prescriptions.

The rational-focused lenses that include presupposed patterns can easily neglect Christian spiritual formation that springs from and attends to a focus on one's heart, soul, and reliance on God's strength. Perhaps a hermeneutic more centered on God, Jesus, and the Spirit can bring needed adjustments to the entrenched pattern that focuses on what to *think* and *do* more than a heart response to the Triune God. Thus, I propose a consideration of lenses that focuses on a theological, redemptive/trajectory, and Spirit hermeneutic to allow greater spiritual formation than the pattern lens allows. While each of these lenses are in some ways rational, they expand beyond "reason" in ways that encourage the formation of the heart.

Adding a Theological Lens: John Mark Hicks

John Mark Hicks, the most prolific contemporary writer on patternism, proposes the addition of a theological hermeneutic to better understand God's character and mission. He explains his view of this hermeneutic:

> These are the two different ways of reading Scripture. One seeks a blueprint pattern for the church to reproduce (which is a function of ecclesiology), and the other seeks the pattern of divine actions (which is, ultimately, a function of Christology). The former seeks conformity to a set of particulars as a measure of the true church, while the latter seeks the embodiment of the life of God among the disciples of Jesus...and divine activity in Christ by the Spirit.[195]

Hicks believes that a theological hermeneutic seeks to understand the working of God's big picture and His character. While interpretation often divides the adherers of patternism, a theological hermeneutic offers different emphases that tend toward unity. A theological hermeneutic looks for ways the Bible tells readers about God. Studying God's work throughout biblical history, it seeks to guide readers in how to participate in God's mission. It searches the heart of God toward men and women and focuses on how to practice this heart of God in the lives of people today. It finds the big picture story in the narrative of Scripture. This view can be resilient and not overly affected by culture. When one views Scripture by searching for who God is, everything is relevant. Hicks continues, explaining that "the rule and canon by which Christians walk is not fundamentally or foundationally the New Testament as a written document but the mighty act of God in Jesus by the Spirit."[196] The criterion of the gospel is what God has done through creation, His promise to Abraham, His covenant with Israel, and the incarnation of Jesus, who remains the hope and salvation of the world. Thus, to be spiritually formed, one must pay attention to the acts of God from beginning to end, creation to new creation.[197] In

---

195. John Mark Hicks, "Searching For the Pattern," *Teleios: A Journal to Promote Holistic Spirituality,* Vol 5, No 1 (2023): 74.

196. John Mark Hicks, *Searching for the Pattern: My Journey in Interpreting the Bible* (Nashville, TN: John Mark Hicks, 2019), Kindle edition, 94.

197. John Mark Hicks, *Searching,* Kindle, 97.

sum, a theological hermeneutic reads the Bible to learn the heart, nature, and work of God, Jesus, and the Holy Spirit.[198]

While most Christian readings incorporate a theological reading of Scripture, Hick's explanation of theological reading contrasts the pattern hermeneutic by focusing on the "who" of the Scriptures above the "what" and "how." The "what" and "how" emphasized in patternism too often miss the relational story of Scripture, thus encourage dogmatic readings and responses. Church communities form and grow from the ways communities read and teach Scripture.

Migliore, expounding on systematic theology pens, "The work of theology is inseparably bound to an identifiable faith community that worships God, attends to Scripture and its account of God's work and will, and engages in manifold ministries of education, reconciliation, and liberation."[199] He notes that communities' quest for truth requires continual critical reflection lest it be "threatened by shallowness, arrogance, and ossification."[200]

Hicks highlights this connection using an example in 2 Cor 9:13-15. "...Through the testing of this ministry you glorify God by your *obedience to the confession of the gospel of Christ* and by the generosity of your sharing with them and others." The obedience Paul describes is not following a blueprint pattern but obedience to the gospel of Christ. Hicks explains that their obedience is not a test of loyalty to a group or some line in the sand about whether a congregation is a true church or not, but rather about whether people believe and internalize the gospel to such an extent that they share their resources with the poor in a way that imitates Christ. "The pattern is not a pattern of prescribed forms...the pattern is Jesus."[201] As a result of this understanding, Hicks shows that theological readers seek to understand:

> *how their story fits into the theological narrative of the text* rather than how the text fits into some larger story. Theological readers do not fuse these horizons of

---

198. John Mark Hicks, *Searching*, Kindle, 91.

199. Daniel L. Migliore, *Fatih Seeking Understanding: An Introduction to Christian Theology* (Grand Rapids, MI: Eerdmans, 2004), xv.

200. Migliore, *Faith Seeking*, xv.

201. John Mark Hicks: "Searching," *Teleios*, 82.

the text's story and our story, but locate themselves within the story of the text. Scripture, or more particularly the narrative of God's activity, is the world we enter in order to discern how to participate in the life and mission of God, which is the life and mission of Jesus.[202]

Hicks provides the language to describe deficiencies of patternism, which often draws lines over details and misses the heart of God. In an effort to find security in obedience, loving God and neighbor was often lost in attempts at precision obedience. In *The Drama of Scripture*, Bartholomew and Goheen respond to a Hindu inquiry of why Christians who claim to believe the Bible have not seen the treasure they have. The authors respond, explaining that:

> ...especially from the pressure of the Enlightenment story, the Bible has been broken up into little bits: historical, critical bits, devotional bits, moral bits, theological bits, narrative bits. In fact, it's been chopped into fragments that fit into the nooks and crannies of the Western cultural story! When this is allowed to happen, the Bible forfeits its claim to be the one comprehensive, true story of our world and is held captive within *another* story—the humanist narrative. And thus it will be that other story that will shape our lives.[203]

Biblical narratives run throughout the Scriptures to tell the big story. Biblical narrative does not bring about clear-cut answers. As Professor Kindalee de Long explains, "Narrative is not law or doctrine. Instead, story raises important questions, gives us examples to consider, creates tensions to wrestle with, and ignites our imaginations. Narrative draws us into conversations that will lead us more deeply into the way of Jesus."[204] The porous meanings derived from poetry and narrative, the most common genres in the Scriptures, are more like peepholes, small openings leading into a larger world.

Along with the strengths of this hermeneutic come accompanying weaknesses that also feed into one's presuppositions. In the story, one can emphasize knowledge over action and thinking

---

202. John Mark Hicks, "Searching," *Teleios*, 84.

203. Craig G. Bartholomew and Michael W. Goheen, *The Drama of Scripture: Finding Our Place in the Biblical Story* (Grand Rapids, MI: Baker Academic, 2014), 22.

204. Kindalee Pfremmer de Long, "Reading Luke's Story of Jesus and the Way," *Teleios: A Journal to Promote Holistic Spirituality* Vol 5, No 1 (2023):19.

about things more than acting on them, becoming too "rational" as well. For this reason, this hermeneutic might appeal to the idealist and contextualist. The strengths bring into focus the heart of God within the Scriptures. If one can view God's desire for His people to be transformed into His image, and since the focus is on God, this can be a powerful hermeneutic for transformation into God's character and mission. When one is immersed in the story of God and embraces His values, this informs and transforms their application of Biblical teachings.

Adding a Redemptive Movement/Trajectory Lens: William J. Webb

William J. Webb, in his writing on *Slaves, Women & Homosexuals: Exploring the Hermeneutics of Cultural Analysis*, offers an additional lens he calls the Redemptive Movement lens, or the Trajectory lens. He offers the explanation:

X = the ethic of the original culture

    Limited movement toward God's ethic

Y = The ethic represented by the isolated words of the biblical text, an ethic frozen in time

Z = Reflected in the spirit of the biblical text, the ultimate ethic[205]

Though Webb comes from a tradition outside of the RM, his observances bring another needed adjustment to the pattern lens. A trajectory lens seeks meaning within the biblical text and canon which is often missed in patternism and other application processes. Webb reminds that "numerous aspects of the biblical text were not written to establish a utopian society with complete justice and equity. They were written within a cultural framework with limited moves toward an ultimate ethic."[206]

Webb explains two approaches for this hermeneutic. One

---

205 Willam J. Webb, *Slaves, Women & Homosexuals: Exploring the Hermeneutics of Cultural Analysis* (Downers Grove, IL: IVP Academic, 2001), 31.

206. Webb, *Slaves*, 31.

interprets the text with a "spirit-movement" component of meaning. This meaning should be prominent for application today. The other approach overlooks the spirit component or devalues its importance for contemporary application.[207] He believes that if the text lays groundwork for further movement in the direction set by the text that would produce a more fully recognized ethic, then that course of action should be pursued.[208]

One might view this interpretive method like an arrow on the way toward its target. It begins in one place but is on a dynamic trajectory toward its goal. If we observe the Bible as a story that has beginning and end, Abraham experiences God in a different way than does Israel.

In the Sermon on the Mount, Jesus reminds the crowd that the law tells them they cannot murder. He shines light on the target, a change of heart that calls them to not get angry. There is a progression of God's will unveiled throughout the Bible. The arrow carries one along as they learn to follow God's path toward His target, which He further sums as loving God with all one's heart, mind, soul, and strength and one's neighbor as themselves (Matthew 22:37-40).

God allows human choice which resulted in polygamy, slavery, patriarchy, primogeniture, kings, wars, and misogyny. God worked His will within the confines of these choices, but His continued teachings and example in Jesus show that these are not His ultimate desire or will. By the time Jesus arrived, polygamy was almost done. In Torah, we see negative examples of polygamy gone awry. Because the love of God means freedom to choose, the created world quickly became ungodly. The journey with God and humans begins first through a chosen person, and then a chosen people worked to build a godly environment out of a chaotic, idolatrous, sinful world. This took time, as God did not force His will on people. Throughout the Old Testament, provisions were made to lead people toward equality and care for one another, but these provisions happened within the culture of the day as God led His people toward His aim. Jesus would call for and demonstrate love

207. Webb, *Slaves*, 34.
208. Webb, *Slaves*, 36.

for one another and self-sacrifice. One could look at scriptures concerning the ways they are to treat their slaves in both the Old Testament and New Testament and assume that God condoned slavery. A pattern hermeneutic, though it once condoned slavery, would ascertain that a modern-day application would involve employees and employers, but some of the instructions would not be applicable.

In my book, *The View from Paul's Window: Paul's Teachings on Women*, I describe the trajectory view:

> What the interpreters of the time seem to have overlooked were broader scriptural principles and the overall trajectory of God's will. They failed to consider the implications of Jesus as the full revelation of God's will (Heb 1:3), a will that had been only partially visible prior to Christ (Heb 1:1-2). They neglected the new paradigm that was created by Jesus' words, urging them to do unto others as they would have done to them (Mt 7:12); they disregarded the call to imitate Christ in putting others' interests ahead of their own (Philippians 2:1-5).[209]

This approach would call one to learn from sins and mistakes of the past and learn God's intent. A pattern hermeneutic seeks to restore the New Testament pattern, but the question must be asked whether God's goal is to restore the New Testament church. That goal becomes problematic in many ways. The early church was replete with problems, which is why the corrective Epistles were written to specific problems in the churches, leading disciples toward a more Christ-like life. This interpretive view considers where might God be taking followers, relying on prayer and the Holy Spirit to take them where they need to go. When one moves forward toward God's intent, barriers from certain people groups will be torn down and people will be seen as equals.

The Redemptive Movement/trajectory hermeneutic focuses on God's intent, His ultimate will. It tends to draw analysts. A valuable tool, it can cause problems when one neglects Scripture in favor of where they desire the trajectory to land. Presuppositions play a role in one's desired outcome. Scripture must be consistent with the rest of the Bible. A weakness of a Redemptive

---

209. Jeanie Shaw, *The View from Paul's Window: Paul's Teachings on Women* (Spring, TX: Illumination Publishers, 2020), 35.

Movement/Trajectory hermeneutic is that one can read conclusions that are not in the text. There can be a temptation to go outside of what is simple and even rewrite God's desires to match one's own. It would seem that putting these aforementioned hermeneutical lenses together would produce more comprehensive and accurate views.

A trajectory hermeneutic becomes a valuable forming tool since the very nature of redemptive movement and trajectory assumes transformation. While a pattern view would dissect the "rules" Paul wrote to Timothy for ecclesial order, a trajectory view would remember Paul's opening words to Timothy. "The goal of this command is love that comes from a pure heart and a good conscience and a sincere faith" (1 Tim 1:5).

A Spirit Hermeneutic: Craig S. Keener

Craig Keener develops a "spirit hermeneutic" that offers a missing link in patternism's rational, one-dimensional interpretation of Scripture. The reason I have chosen Keener to help me develop a three-fold hermeneutic adjustment is that his approach charts a way beyond hampering polarities and binaries such as intellectual/ pietistic, academic/spiritual, cognitive/effective, self-formational/ world-changing, rationalistic/charismatic, speculative-theoretical/ pragmatic-practical, sectarian/ecumenical, and ecclesial/public.[210] Patternism is filled with hampering polarities and binaries.

Keener views his approach as a companion to exegesis, not a replacement. His approach adds essential dimension to the one-dimensional patternism as he states:

> ...we are interested in biblical texts not simply for what they teach us about ancient history or ideas, but because we expect to share the kind of spiritual experience and relationship that we discover in Scripture. Jesus' resurrection is not a mere historical datum; it declares that the Jesus we learn about in the Gospels is now the exalted Lord, who has sent his Spirit so that we may continue to experience his presence.[211]

---

210. Craig S. Keener, *Spirit Hermeneutics: Reading Scripture in Light of Pentecost* (Grand Rapids, MI: Eerdmans, 2016), xxi.

211. Keener, *Spirit*, 5.

Keener believes that "an approach sterilized from any direct faith in the supernatural differs significantly from how the biblical writers intended their works to be read." [212] He assumes that God has a present voice, quoting A.W. Tozer's words, "It is the present Voice which makes the written Word all-powerful." [213] He believes that when one correctly understands the Scriptures, they find numerous instances of divine encounters and a current, living relationship with Christ.

Keener defines Spirit hermeneutic as one that "recognizes in Scripture the prevalence and promise of divine activity, and expecting the Spirit's presence and pedagogy as we read Scripture." [214] He emphasizes a personal encounter, noting that it is one thing to "affirm academically that God loves us. It is another to welcome that truth into our hearts that have felt wounded and untrusting." [215] The pattern hermeneutic requires one to stand off-stage, observing a drama through rational, objective lens of scholarship, all while "the Holy Spirit draws one on stage with the actors." [216] A Spirit hermeneutic "seeks to escape 'unbridled rationalism,' which has tended toward a spiritual dead end in the church's use of Scripture." [217] A Spirit hermeneutic reads Scripture dynamically and relationally. He notes that Pentecostalism was also a restorationist movement. He observes that various forms of restorationism became legalistic, exalting their group over another. [218]

Like the theological and trajectory hermeneutic, a Spirit hermeneutic points toward a fuller picture of God, wrestling with texts "in light of what we know of God's heart until we better understand its point." [219] Looking at Scripture through the lens of God's heart compels people toward His concern for people and their needs, thus forming a deeper sense of unity and mission. One must then rely on the Spirit to empower them to help meet each other's needs.

---

212. Keener, *Spirit*, 11.
213. Keener, *Spirit*, 14.
214. Keener, *Spirit*, 18.
215. Keener, *Spirit*, 25.
216. Keener, *Spirit*, 41.
217. Keener, *Spirit*, 84.
218. Keener, *Spirit*, 27.
219. Keener, *Spirit*, 42.
220. Keener, *Spirit*, 48.

A strength of the Spirit hermeneutic is the way it fosters dependence on God rather than self. This demand requires humility. Keener notes that "the humble read Scripture not simply to reinforce their knowledge, but with desperation and/or faith to hear God there. They read with dependence on God, trusting the Holy Spirit to lead them."[221] It also energizes believers as they encounter a living, dynamic presence of God. Any hermeneutic that encourages humility and relational dynamics feeds formation toward becoming more like Christ, and by finding relational fulfilment in Him it also affects human relationships.

Weaknesses in the Spirit hermeneutic include the possibilities of misconstruing the voice of the Spirit with other voices vying for attention—self, secular, and the Evil one. These voices seek to distort God's will, yet the voice of the Spirit will not contradict God's will found in His Word. This approach can tempt one to value experience over God's written Word. However, patternism often assumes one or the other, devaluing experience.

Since the Spirit lives in the Christian, the Spirit must not be ignored, and it is vital to know that the Bible and the Spirit are not the same thing. If the Spirit is ignored, or as Francis Chan describes, becomes the "forgotten God,"[221] Christians will feel empty and eventually burn out. While they may still be bound by duty, they fail to experience the strengthening with power through His Spirit in their inner being through "his glorious riches" (Eph 3:16).

Feelers, artists, and relationally intuitive persons may be more drawn to this hermeneutic, along with those who feel dry spiritually. Each of these lenses can serve to bring greater clarity to interpretation, like the "second touch" from Jesus to the man whose newly found vision was still blurred.

Comparative Analysis of Four Hermeneutics

To better understand the formative influence of hermeneutics, I offer a passage of Scripture in Ephesians 5:21-6:9, highlighting the emphases that each hermeneutic offers with the resulting formational tendencies.

---

221. Francis Chan and Danae Yankoski, *Forgotten God: Reversing Our Tragic Neglect of the Holy Spirit* (Colorado Springs, CO: David Cook, 2009).

Submit to one another out of reverence for Christ. Wives, submit yourselves to your own husbands as you do to the Lord. For the husband is the head of the wife as Christ is the head of the church, his body, of which he is the Savior. Now as the church submits to Christ, so also wives should submit to their husbands in everything. Husbands, love your wives, just as Christ loved the church and gave himself up for her to make her holy, cleansing her by the washing with water through the word, and to present her to himself as a radiant church, without stain or wrinkle or any other blemish, but holy and blameless. In this same way, husbands ought to love their wives as their own bodies. He who loves his wife loves himself. After all, no one ever hated their own body, but they feed and care for their body, just as Christ does the church—for we are members of his body. "For this reason a man will leave his father and mother and be united to his wife, and the two will become one flesh." This is a profound mystery—but I am talking about Christ and the church. However, each one of you also must love his wife as he loves himself, and the wife must respect her husband. Children, obey your parents in the Lord, for this is right. "Honor your father and mother"—which is the first commandment with a promise—"so that it may go well with you and that you may enjoy long life on the earth." Fathers, do not exasperate your children; instead, bring them up in the training and instruction of the Lord. Slaves, obey your earthly masters with respect and fear, and with sincerity of heart, just as you would obey Christ. Obey them not only to win their favor when their eye is on you, but as slaves of Christ, doing the will of God from your heart. Serve wholeheartedly, as if you were serving the Lord, not people, because you know that the Lord will reward each one for whatever good they do, whether they are slave or free. And masters, treat your slaves in the same way. Do not threaten them, since you know that he who is both their Master and yours is in heaven, and there is no favoritism with him. (NIV, 2011)

Ephesians 5:21–6:9	Emphases	Forming Tendencies
Pattern	The rules of the household are clear. Though all are to have submissive hearts, in a marriage the husband is the head, or authority. The wife is to be submissive, and the husband should practice benevolent authority. Children are to be obedient to their parents, and slaves (usually interpreted today as employees) to their masters (employers) as unto Christ. Emphasizes Jesus as subservient to God for all time, and marriage as the illustration of hierarchical roles.	This hierarchical view tempts the one with authority toward power and to view the other as less than, even though theologically this would be argued. Often, as has been shown, power goes awry. Human nature tends toward entitlement practiced by the one holding power. While the hierarchical roles can produce good, functional marriages, both spouses practicing self-sacrifice and submission toward the other more accurately mirrors the way of Christ. In hierarchical roles, the woman may not recognize or use her gifts to the full, believing her main function is to complete the spouse. This ordering of roles often includes roles in the church, thus limiting women's use of gifts in the church. Respect is often taught as necessary for a husband to receive, but not the wife. Love can be seen as necessary for the wife to feel, but not the husband. This interpretation can tend toward one's view of God more as an authoritative figure than one who desires an intimate relationship.
Theological	Jesus loves in a self-sacrificing way. God imparts holiness to us. Christ cares for the church, His people. He unites us with Him as His own body. We are nurtured by and through Him as He allows us to be one with Him. The Lord rewards everyone. God has no favoritism. The Scripture describes the unity between Christ and His people. Marriage is just an analogy. Mutual submission is demonstrated as Christ emptied Himself and submitted to the cross for our sake as He emptied Himself, becoming human so we could become divine (*kenosis*).	A focus on self-sacrifice and nurturing feeds "the other" more than self. The focus is not on who is in charge but rather a Philippians 2 (emptying of self) perspective. The view of God as a rewarder helps one see God as one who is for them rather than living in fear of messing up. A focus on God who has no favoritism begets humility and minimizes entitlement. This focus brings hope that no matter how unfairly one is treated, God sees, rewards, and shows no favoritism.

Ephesians 5:21–6:9	Emphases	Forming Tendencies
Trajectory	Paul works within the cultural ANE household codes, moving Christians forward in profound ways. He addresses wives, children, and slaves. This was abnormal, in a culture that considered them property. His charge for a husband to leave father and mother would have been radical in the deeply embedded patriarchal culture. Emphasis would observe where might God be taking His people. . . relying on Holy Spirit and prayer to take them where they need to go. Observes where barriers from certain people groups would be torn down and people would view one another as equals. It subverts the cultural mode by the model that appears, pointing to something even fuller in the light of Christ.	This hermeneutic puts one in a learner mode rather than having truth "wrapped up in their back pocket." If one believes God is aiming them toward something higher, then they must be looking for His lead and to be assured that they still have growing to do. This fosters a desire to learn from others and to invite other perspectives, since God is moving us along a path. This view encourages a journey mindset rather than one of arrival. This journey reminds of the need to receive and give grace.
Spirit	God's Spirit is a Spirit of unity. The Triune God shows us unity. The scripture describes this unity of the Spirit as one flesh, using the metaphor of the unity of head and body. A decapitated head from body is not a mystery. Hierarchy is not a mystery. The Triune God is a mystery, and unity is a mystery. The Spirit makes this known in ways impossible for humankind to accomplish without the union of humankind with God's Spirit.	Since the Spirit is still alive and well and leads us, dependency on God becomes more important, and self-reliance becomes less. This new way of thinking and being cannot be achieved by human effort alone. This posture elevates faith in God more than humanistic "figuring things out." This brings peace, knowing one does not have to figure everything out and be in control, needing to "make it happen."

All four of these hermeneutical lenses have specific emphases and forming tendencies. The exercise of working backwards (by observing the things one emphasizes and the accompanying forming tendencies) can shed light on the ways one most often interprets Scripture. Problems arise when one believes that their approach to Scripture is the only way it can be viewed. Through awareness and the melding of different lenses one can reframe or replace a long-held pattern hermeneutic, using a more complete lens prescription that results in clearer vision.

When a person recognizes their own presuppositions and is willing to try new, more comprehensive lenses, they gain increased clarity and greater transformation into the image of Christ. The Apostle John adjusted his lens as he grew in Christ. As a young disciple, when he saw others not doing things "the right way" he desired to call down fire from heaven to destroy them (Luke 9:53-56). As he watched and learned through the eyes of Jesus, he heard Jesus' reaction as told in Mark 9:38-41, a scripture that patternists would likely find difficult:

> "Teacher," said John, "we saw someone driving out demons in your name and we told him to stop, because he was not one of us." "Do not stop him," Jesus said. "For no one who does a miracle in my name can in the next moment say anything bad about me, for whoever is not against us is for us. Truly I tell you, anyone who gives you a cup of water in my name because you belong to the Messiah will certainly not lose their reward.

John, in later years, not only penned the "love epistles" of his last three letters, but was known as the Apostle of love. Tradition tells that as he grew old and feeble, others would help him up to speak, and the poignant words he spoke were always, "Love one another."

Conclusion: Melding Lenses for Clarity

Since everyone comes to the table with presuppositions and personality traits, it can be freeing to illuminate the markers, strengths, weaknesses, and formative nature of our preferred hermeneutic. Until one becomes self-aware of their hermeneutic and accompanying formative values that their hermeneutic encourages or discourages, they are likely to miss personal and scriptural blind spots, thus impairing their vision.

While I have critiqued the pattern hermeneutic most severely because it remains embedded in many RM churches and hinders formation, it still offers an important emphasis on obeying Scripture, though it does so through an incomplete and often distorted lens. The principles that pertain to Christlike, holy living are not difficult to understand, though often difficult to practice. The ecclesial perfection sought from patterns, inferences, and examples in the New Testament misses the mark of spiritual formation. When one presumes certainty while interpreting New Testament letters that were written for us but not to us and assigns their certainty as dogma, formation takes an un-Christlike turn.[222]

While blueprints are needed to begin building, they must be adjusted as they are built upon. The cornerstone of faith will always be Jesus, and the prophets and apostles are part of the foundation meant to create unity in His holy temple, the church, where He lives in His people through the Spirit (Eph 2:19-21). Unfortunately, as churches matured in the RM, interpretation methods often did not mature and became legalistic. Before adjustments to interpretation can happen, one must accept the reality of more than one approach in interpreting Scripture. This becomes challenging for one who believes that the patterns they see in Scripture are the

---

222. To illustrate just how difficult it can be to interpret letters written to specific situations across generations and cultures, I asked my (then) eighteen-year-old granddaughter to write a letter to a peer concerning her grade on an assignment from her teacher. Imagine the difficulty in interpretation if this letter could be teleported across time and distance to the Ancient Middle East. Enjoy: "Yo, my teacher was being such a force today. Like bruh, no wonder she ain't cuffed yet, she's legit such a Karen. She said I'd lose 20 points off my grade for submitting my report a MINUTE late. I thought she was capping but turns out she was spitting facts, so I had to finesse it using spark notes. I lowkey thought the paper turned out fire after doe. Went to the mall so I could flex on the class how professional I looked for the report presentation. Then went to present it in class the next day, drowning in my new drip, looking SNATCHED, but the teacher was acting so sus. My presentation was sick tho so idk why she was being sketch. Bad vibes all around, no cap. She legit didn't look up once from her desk while I presented, then gave me a 60. Like bruh, I was mad salty. Idk why she was throwing sm shade so then I called her out after class. Turns out she didn't think my dope fit was "appropriate attire" smh because it was too casual?? I literally looked so dope tho, like mom jeans and a crew neck give boss vibes only tbh. Like if you saw the fit, I think you'd ship me with Harry Styles over you. I pointed out the rubric NEVER said attire mattered and then she finessed my grade after. Savage moves only for dis queen, PERIODT. grade is all gucci now, and next class is lit so we vibing. next teacher is the goat. I think that's all the tea but I'll keep da squad posted if teacher rages at me anymore, pce out fam."

only right possibilities. Dogma and ecclesial perfectionism accompany this stance. Each of the four hermeneutics discussed are tethered to Scripture and carry needed aspects of interpretation. Together, they sharpen the focus on loving God with all one's heart, mind, soul, and strength. If the theological, redemptive/trajectory, and pneumatic lenses can be melded, blind spots will be minimized, vision can become clearer, and unity can become more of a reality. The questions one brings to their Bible study will impact the answers they find, and one's approach to Scripture affects their formation into the image of Christ. The relationship between one's hermeneutic and their spiritual formation remains indelibly intertwined. Patternism by itself is incomplete, tending to one's mind and actions, but often missing the heart and power behind the living Word.

223

---

223. Illustration by Seluk Erdem

CHAPTER FOUR

Adding a 3-D Lens: The Relationship between Restoration Movement Hermeneutics, the Spirit, and Experiencing God

Is it not true that for most of us who call ourselves Christians there is no real experience? We have substituted theological ideas for an arresting encounter, we are full of religious notions, but our great weakness is that for our hearts there is no one there. Whatever else it embraces, true Christian experience must always include a genuine encounter with God. Without this, religion is but a shadow, a reflection of reality, a cheap copy of an original once enjoyed by someone else of whom we have heard.[224]

The Restoration Movement's eagerness to "restore New Testament Christianity"[225] through its rational understanding of sound doctrine[226] built from commands, examples, and inferences often restricted the Holy Spirit's "unreasonable" work beyond the Scriptures. This resulted in a focus on the "Father, Son, and the Holy Scriptures."[227] The view through this lens, combined with

---

224. W. Tozer, *God's Pursuit of Man: Tozer's Profound Prequel to The Pursuit of God* (Chicago: Moody Publishers, 1950, 1978), 18-19.

225. A common mantra used by Restoration Movement leaders as quoted in chapter one.

226. The word translated "sound" *(hugiainō)* is translated every time in the Pastorals this way in the NASB, and yet the word itself means "healthy." Hence, sound teaching is teaching that makes one spiritually healthy. Then you have the second word, doctrine *(didaskalia)*, translated 9 of 15 times in the Pastorals as doctrine in the NASB. Yet, how does an English dictionary define doctrine? The Cambridge English Dictionary has this: "a belief or set of beliefs, especially political or religious ones, that are taught and accepted by a particular group." When you are indoctrinated with an approach to interpretation with its foundation in pattern theology, sound doctrine will come to mean a type of important or essential theological doctrines and much of it will fall into the category of salvation essentials. When doctrine is exalted to such a status, it will end up being shocking in what will be included under the banner of salvation matters. It is, in fact, quite shocking when you study the history of the RM. But this word doctrine in the Greek is simply the normal word for teaching. Sound doctrine is healthy teaching, no more and no less.

227. M. James Sawyer, "The Father, the Son, and the Holy Scriptures?" in Daniel B. Wallace and M. James Sawyer, eds., *Who's Afraid of the Holy Spirit?: An Investigation into the Ministry of the Spirit of God Today* (Dallas: Biblical Studies Press, 2013), 253-77.

the stark contrast between contemporary Western culture and the Ancient Near Eastern culture of the Bible, makes it nearly impossible for those in Western cultures to perceive and engage the working of the Spirit.[228] Throughout the Bible, the Spirit has always done what the Spirit wants to do, when it wants to do it, and how it wants to do it. New Testament scholar Scot McKnight writes of the need for greater openness to the Spirit stating, "some Christians are so Bible-focused they seem to forget that God is not the Bible. God is a Person, and the Bible is paper. But the paper becomes the voice of the Person only when we are open to the Holy Spirit."[229]

To read the Bible beyond a one or two-dimensional literal reading requires an anaglyph (3D) lens that looks to a dimension beyond pure reason to essential movement, thrust, and experience, all necessary to sustain one for their Christian life journey.[230] The rational, pragmatic hermeneutic of the Restoration Movement often neglects Spirit-led, experiential encounters between God and humanity, thus marginalizing the foundational heart/relational connections where formation into the image of Christ takes root.

The History of the Spirit in the Text

The role of the Spirit of God looms large in RM interpretation and serves as the backdrop for understanding ways one "experiences" God. Leaders in RM history long debated the working of the Spirit in a Christian's life. Some taught that the Spirit worked only through the Word of God,[231] yet the Bible contains many examples showing that the Spirit lives beyond the pages of the Bible.

---

228. Donald K. Smith, "The Holy Spirit in Missions," in Daniel B. Wallace and James Sawyer, eds., *Who's Afraid of the Holy Spirit?: An Investigation into the Ministry of the Spirit of God Today* (Dallas: Biblical Studies Press, 2013), 244.

229. Scot McKnight, *Open to the Spirit: God in Us, God with Us, and God Transforming Us* (NY: Waterbrook, 2018), 28.

230. In movie theatres, anaglyph lenses allow people to view in 3D. I use this term to refer to an extra-dimensional lens, one not visible to flattened, one-dimensional views.

231. Alexander Campbell, "The Voice of God and the Word of God," *Millennial Harbinger*, Vol 1 (1830): 127-8. Campbell states, "'Tis in it the Spirit of God exhibits his energy, and he who thinks that the Spirit operates in any other way than clothed in the word of God in convincing and converting the world, feeds upon a fancy of his own, or of some other distempered mind."

A glance through biblical history shows that Noah, Abraham, and Moses experienced God without the Bible. The kings and prophets only had the law, but David and the other psalmists certainly experienced God apart from Scripture. In the New Testament, Mary experienced God, as did Peter, Paul, and John. The Psalms often tell of the ever-present God. God's Spirit promises to direct, teach, comfort, guide, lead to understanding, speak with God, and to see things beyond the physical.[232] The Bible and a relationship with God are not the same thing. One cannot have a relationship with a text.

As the history of our early church leaders and even recent church leaders shows, the RM churches have often entered that slippery slope of self-reliance rather than dependence on the Spirit of God. Though some second and third generation RM leaders advanced the "Spirit contained in the Bible" interpretation, some of the RM founding fathers allowed room for the Spirit. Barton Stone spoke much more about the Spirit than did Alexander Campbell. Stone advised, "A Christian cannot exist without the Bible, God's Word, but neither can one exist without the Spirit of God. He declared, "some appear to make the Scriptures everything in regeneration; and others make them nothing."[233] He considered both of these opinions as extreme.

Stone's autobiography showed his belief in the importance of firsthand Christian experience. He believed it possible for the Holy Spirit to enlighten and guide one in the study of the Word of God apart from the traditional creeds of Christendom. In contrast, Campbell wrote to the editor of the *Baptist Interpreter*. "...how the Spirit operates in the Word, through the Word, by the Word, or with the Word, I do not affirm. I only oppose the idea that anyone is changed in heart or renewed in the spirit of his mind by the Spirit without the Word."[234] This clarifies Campbell's view that the Scriptures contained the Holy Spirit, and without the Word, the Spirit was not operative in one's life. This view restricts spiritual

---

232. John 14:16, 26; 15:26; 16:13; Eph 5:18; Acts 1:8; Rom 8:26; Ps 119:18-19.

233. Donald M. Kinder, *Capturing Head and Heart* (Abilene, TX: Abilene Christian University Press, Kindle edition), 71.

234. Murch, *Christians Only*, 117.

formation outside of a "boxed" Bible.

Robert Richardson, who authored the memoirs of Alexander Campbell and noted the elevation of arguments and debates over meditation on the character of Christ and one's own state, did not believe the Spirit was limited to facts about the gospel contained in the first century document.[235] He believed, though nature cannot bring one to repentance, it can bring one closer to their creator. He believed the Spirit moved in spheres of divine proclamation and is instrumental in God's response to prayers. Richardson was known as "an oasis of spirituality in a time when 'heartless and superficial formalism' was overtaking the movement."[236]

Opposing schools of interpretive thought concerning the Spirit of God became issues throughout RM history. One view taught that the Spirit was fully contained in the Scriptures which were inspired by God and gave everything needed "for life and godliness" (2 Pet 1:3), and the other view saw the Spirit at work beyond the biblical text. This controversy highlighted the clash of incompatible theologies of two editors, Richardson with the *Millennial Harbinger* and Tolbert Fanning, with the *Gospel Advocate*. Richardson "insisted that the Spiritual truth contained in the Bible must be received, not merely with understanding, but with the spirit and heart."[237] Fanning would argue that the Spirit is contained in the Bible. Richardson and Campbell would also differ on this understanding. Campbell's Lockean views of faith were built "in opposition to what he considered extreme and damaging views of 'spiritual operations.'"[238] Richardson believed that "such a definition makes faith little more than an intellectual assent to the truthfulness of facts rather than trust in a person...and this was paralyzing the movement's Spiritual progress."[239] Richardson also implied the centrality of the doctrine of the Trinity to reveal a "God who is dynamic, demanding, personal, and present."

---

235. Kinder, *Capturing Head & Heart*, 34.

236. Kinder, *Capturing Head and Heart*, 35.

237. C. Leonard Allen and Danny Gray Swick, *Participating in God's Life: Two Crossroads for Churches of Christ* (Orange, CA: New Leaf Books, 2001), 37-38.

238. Allen, *Participating in God's Life*, 45.

239. Allen, *Participating in God's Life*, 45.

RM scholar and author Leonard Allen sees this doctrine extremely lacking in the churches of Christ that weaken, neglect, or distort this doctrine.[240] Ultimately, Campbell's and Fanning's ideologies would win the day. When the debate of the Spirit's role in interpretation re-arose in the RM churches in the 1960's, this entrenched philosophy had already been lurking behind the scenes at an unconscious, ideological level ever since Richardson's and Fanning's conflicting theologies came to light a century earlier.[241] The Spirit was, the "Forgotten God."

The view which contained and limited the Spirit fit well with patternism's dependence on certainty. With a contained Spirit, one can gain mastery and control of the Word. The Spirit contained in the Word takes away the unknown. Self-reliance replaces Spirit-reliance, which would be too mysterious and unpredictable for patternists. This self-reliance versus Spirit direction produced and produces far-reaching effects on formation that has evolved throughout RM history.

John Rogers, who had assisted in the union of the Stone and Campbell movements, wrote to Alexander Campbell in 1834: "Many of us, in running away from the extreme of enthusiasm, have, on the other hand, passed the temperate zone, and gone far into the frozen regions...There is in too many churches, a cold-hearted, lifeless formality that freezes the energies." Here, he suggests that fear of enthusiasm may have caused the reduction in heart.[242]

While the ICOC seldom lacks in enthusiasm or is accused of superficial formalism, only recently has more attention been given to the Spirit of God as an entity of God that "blows where it will" and leads into unknowns (John 3:8). Strategizing and planning, while often needed, still easily take center stage leading to personality and self-dependent trajectories.

Using analogies of militaristic advances for the mission of Christ, Kip McKean, who was raised by a Navy admiral, practiced a military model of leadership in the ICOC. This model offered a

---

240. Allen, *Participating in God's Life*, 56.
241. Allen, *Participating in God's Life*, 56.
242. Kinder, *Capturing Head and Heart*, 20.

plethora of precision obedience and certainty practices.[243] Military models "make things happen" and legal models apply the letter of the law. Numerous examples can be seen throughout Scripture of God's displeasure with "making it happen" rather than waiting and listening for the Spirit of God. The tower of Babel and the day of Pentecost contrast this difference. The former sought to "make it happen" and the latter stood in awe of the transforming Spirit at work. Only by the Spirit can one be continually transformed into the image of Christ (2 Cor. 3:17-18).

The Spirit of the Word

While the Spirit will never negate or contradict God's Word, the Spirit cannot be contained between the bound cover of the Bible. The patternist would contain the Spirit in the Bible and assume those with broader interpretation are not taking Scripture seriously. Throughout the RM, the working of the Spirit was a dividing issue. The Spirit, however, is a unifier.[244] Patternism often missed the Spirit while seeking to apply the text, and this missing link was often accompanied by fear. Yet, without the working of the Spirit, both individual and communal spiritual formation and experience ran dry.

Transformation into the image of Christ includes growth in love, joy, peace, patience, gentleness, and all fruits of the Spirit. It must also include the broader community—how one treats the poor, immigrants, those outside one's ethnicity or gender, and how one cares for God's creation. As Jack Levison expounds, "The spirit (life-giving breath of God) is in every human, the spirit is present in social upheaval, the spirit inspires whole communities, inspires ecstasy and restraint, study and spontaneity, and drives the faithful into areas of hostility."[245]

---

243. This could be seen in excessive accountability (red books), and formulas for how many people would need to be contacted to make a convert. Every person was seen as someone to convert, someone on their way to hell. The Spirit was taught in the study series, but more in relation to what the Spirit does not do, and to refute the charismatic gifts.

244. Eph 4:1-4; 1 Cor 6:17; 1 Cor 12:13; 2 Cor 13:14; Php 1:27; Php 2:2.

245. Jack Levison, *Fresh Air: The Holy Spirit for an Inspired Life* (Brewster, MA: Paraclete Press, 2012), 10. Levison uses lower-case "spirit" to distinguish between the breath of life given to each person when created in the image of God and the Spirit as an entity of God.

The Restoration Movement's default hermeneutic must add a lens that encourages adherers to see beyond a two-dimensional focus on Christian doctrine and life to a third dimension, the living Spirit that cannot be mastered or contained. This lens will expose a more experiential and sustainable spiritual formation and discipleship. Unless time and attention are given to add an anaglyph lens of the Spirit which views God beyond the written page, spiritual formation, including the church's unity and mission, cannot be sustained.

Applying the Text but Missing the Spirit

One of the great strengths of the Restoration Movement is its love of the Word. Orthodoxy remains crucial for one's ability to know God, for the Scriptures teach one cannot know or be known by God without obedience to God's Word accompanied by godly living (1 Jn 2:3-6). Though excellent exegesis and right actions may be employed through patternism, unless interpretive methods transform one toward the heart of Jesus, they remain incomplete. Without engaging the Spirit, the Bible becomes rules, moral axioms, or a movement more than a relationship with the One who Christians are called to follow. Formation then follows a system, rather than the Spirit.

The Bible's commands and guides for living point humanity to the ever-present God who desires relationship more than a pattern for New Testament Christianity. When adding an anaglyph lens that views and engages the Spirit, one reads not only to understand what is said in the original context. In addition, the Spirit penetrates the words onto one's heart, enabling deeper spiritual formation. The Spirit can empower one to receive God's message, understanding not just what the Bible says, but what it means. Patternism falls short of this step, impeding a deepening, continued formation. Patternists often miss this step out of various fears, particularly since patternism often stems from a fear-based view of God.

Recognizing a fear-based heart blockage

The Restoration Movement's tendency toward perfectionism

leads one to view God as a scrutinizer of perfection. When people see God this way, their views toward others become judgmental and dogmatic. This perspective thwarts transformation into God's image, so much so that it even affects the physical body. Timothy Jennings, a medical doctor who researched the physical and spiritual connection between one's view of God and transformation notes, "...when we worship a god other than one of love—a being who is punitive, authoritarian, critical, or distant—fear circuits are activated and, if not calmed, will result in chronic inflammation and damage to both body and brain. As we bow before authoritarian gods, our characters are slowly changed to be less like Jesus."[246] Thus, when one dogmatically holds to doctrine without understanding the heart of God as demonstrated in Jesus and continued by the Spirit, their spiritual and physical lives suffer.

Since rational doctrine characterizes the pattern hermeneutic, many of those raised in pattern theology fear viewing through a multi-dimensional, anaglyph lens. Currently in the ICOC, discussions on the role of women in the church have produced various degrees of fear—fear of change and fear of straying from the pattern.[247] New ways of thinking and experiencing can become suspect. Those holding to long-held patterns can fear that offering credibility to experience will negate or mar reason.

Fear of uncertainty

Pattern interpretations of Scripture accept the fact that Jesus taught that true worshipers must worship in Spirit and truth, but truth gets the front seat. With this perspective, when something is not recorded in book, chapter, and verse as we read, the Spirit's

---

246. Andrew Newberg and Mark Robert Waldman, *How God Changes Your Brain: Breakthrough Findings from a Leading Neurologist* (New York: Random House, 2009), 19-20, 36-39, 53 cited in Timothy Jennings, M.D., *The God-Shaped Brain* (Downers Grove, IL: Inter-Varsity Press, 2017), 27.

247. In 2020 leadership discussions began in the International Churches of Christ concerning the role of women teaching and preaching in the church. That same year three books were published from the ICOC and the churches of Christ. *Women Serving God,* challenging some long-held understandings, was published by Professor John Mark Hicks of Lipscomb University, a Church of Christ university. The ICOC teachers' task force (of which I was a part) published an exegetical, academic survey of the most debated NT scriptures concerning women, and the ICOC publishing arm, Illumination Publishers, also published a book I wrote called, *The View from Paul's Window: Paul's Teachings on Women,* which I refrained from publishing for two years until the teachers had done their study.

involvement is questionable. Anything viewed outside of a pattern in the New Testament becomes viewed with suspicion, thus creating a culture that fears the Spirit and forms a fear-based "relationship" with God and others. Two well-known theologians extrapolate on reasons fundamentalists fear experiencing God. Believing that theologians have substituted reason for revelation, James Draper, former president of the Southern Baptist Convention, articulates this fear of acknowledging experience as a reliable source of formation:

When one takes that tragic step, the result is usually a loss of mission and evangelistic zeal; theological defection; undue emphasis upon the material and temporal with a corresponding loss of consciousness of the eternal; reliance upon mystical, personal truth; unjustified attachment to human reasoning—to name but a few spiritually destructive positions.[248]

He continues with his premise that this is an epistemological issue.

In response, theologian William Abraham sums several flaws he views in Fundamentalist doctrine of Scripture. "It historically depended on a doctrine of divine dictation or a confusing of divine inspiration with divine speaking and related speech acts of God; the move to include inerrancy of Scripture a key church creed."[249]

Abraham views this as a radical departure from the "actual canonical decisions of the church" and a profound reorientation of the inner structure of the church's intellectual heritage and vision, shifting from soteriology to epistemology. He believes the crux of the church's life stems from the exploration of the full riches of God through Christ in the flesh and through the agency of the Spirit. He sees humility and radical openness to "meeting and receiving" the living God as the beginning and ending of renewal.[250] These characteristics step out of rational, pragmatic comfort zones, so an integration of experience and rational thought must be carefully considered when introducing them to long held patternists. New lenses may feel strange.

248. James Draper, *Authority: The Critical Issue for Southern Baptists* (Old Tappan, NJ: Revell, 1984). 35

249. William J Abraham, *The Divine Inspiration of Holy Scripture* (Oxford: Oxford Univ Press, 1981), 4.

250. Abraham, *The Divine Inspiration*, 5.

Rational Restoration Movement interpretation likes certainty, and experience challenges certainty. After all, the Apostle John tells us the Spirit blows where it will and cannot be contained. Writing on this premise, Peter Enns opines:

> We have misunderstood faith as a what word rather than a who word...The life of Christian faith is more than agreeing with a set of beliefs about Christ, morality, or how to read the Bible. It means being so intimately connected to Christ that his crucifixion is ours, his death is our death, and his life is our life—which is hardly something we can grasp with our minds. It has to be experienced. [251]

Some of the early twentieth century RM leaders understood this connection: James A. Harding, co-founder of Lipscomb University, evangelist, and debater wrote:

> Not a few people seem to be under the impression that all divine interventions have ceased since the death of the apostles, and that since then there have been no supermundane or super-human influences known on earth. They think God gave the word and stopped—a very low and very erroneous conception of the reign of Christ. [252]

This connection, however, was dim throughout most of Restoration history and remains anemic in current teaching. The RM's tendency toward dogmatic certainty in interpretation tends to downplay experiences that cannot be rationally measured. This resistance may come from fear or from lack of understanding of Jesus' focus on relationships formed by the Spirit. Without a belief in and focus on the Spirit of God, Christianity can be whittled to an adherence to biblical patterns, self-help axioms, or what Andrew Root describes as "an epistemological shift rather than an ontological encounter."[253] The implications on spiritual formation are profound. The pattern lens tends toward a head-centered "relationship" that can become rote, or even oppressive, if the Spirit

251. Peter Enns, *The Sin of Certainty: Why God Desires Our Trust More than our "Correct" Beliefs* (San Francisco, CA: Harper One, 2016), 162.

252. James A. Harding, "Prayer for the Sick," *The Way* 3.6 (9 May 1901): 41.

253. Andrew Root, *Faith Formation in a Secular Age* (Grand Rapids, MI: Baker Academics, 2017), 83.

is not awakened. As a result, adherers often either settle for a form of religion or hunger for more.

A Desire for More: A Need for 3D lenses

When the 2020 pandemic hit, like other churches, the ICOC was forced to move online. Members were able to access teaching beyond their individual congregations. Several ICOC teachers who had experienced benefits of spiritual formation and spiritual disciplines began offering online spiritual formation classes for members. In one such class, the response was so large that one class became three. In another, the Zoom platform had to be increased to access up to five hundred people. Near the end of one such class, the presenter sent a questionnaire to its several hundred participants, all from ICOC churches throughout numerous states and countries. They were asked how the spiritual, experiential formation from the heart they had been learning differed from their traditional understandings of formation (or discipleship). A sampling of answers, many of which echoed the same thoughts include:

- Discipleship was more about measuring performance while transformation encourages us to learn how to effectively engage with God so that we become what he created us to be individually and collectively.
- I've found that embracing the experience of God much more restorative and life-giving in comparison to taking a scripture, understanding it, recognizing my faults, and immediately applying it to my life. No meditation, but simple obedience like with a boss.
- Discipleship could be sensed as hierarchical at times or otherwise have a militaristic bent, where transformation has a feeling of being led by God to respond because of my knowledge of His love for me.[254]

Robust participation in opportunities such as these points to a hunger and thirst for something more, as members expressed their desires for a deeper, more heartfelt relationship with God. The Spirit supplies that "something more," and is essential to

---

254. A survey was sent to 304 participants of a 12-week online presentation with the ICOC of "Forming: A Work of Grace," on February 1, 2022. 77 responded. These responses are representative samplings.

comfort, sustain, direct, and take one's longings or groans to God. Daniel Wallace, professor of New Testament studies at Dallas Theological Seminary, in response to his eight-year-old son's cancer diagnosis gave language to this "need for more:"

> I found that the Bible was not adequate. I needed God in a personal way—not as an object of my study, but as friend, guide, comforter. I needed an existential experience of the Holy One. Quite frankly, I found the Bible was not the answer. I found the Scriptures to be helpful—even authoritatively helpful—as a guide. But without feeling God, the Bible gave me little solace. . . I longed for him, but found many community wide restrictions in my cessasionist environment. I looked for God, but all I found was a suffocation of the Spirit in my evangelical tradition as well as in my own heart.[255]

Wallace's words echo the survey responses. Without a "third-dimensional" lens that can deepen one's interpretive lens, the one-dimensional pattern interpretation leaves one longing for more.

Integrating Relationship and Experience

How does one who employs the doctrine and practice derived from their patternistic hermeneutic add heart and spirit to their interpretive lens while still respecting the authority of Scripture? This addition requires that one understands God's desire for relationship is foundational for spiritual formation, moving one outside of the confines of a pattern. In the Ancient Near East, "knowing" was relational and experiential. For example, the Hebrew word for "know" was often used for sexual intercourse, and intimate experience.[256] To undergird orthodoxy and orthopraxy with the breath and wind of the moving Spirit (Hebrew *ruach*, Greek *pneum*), a relational lens of interpretation becomes imperative. Without the lens of a relational encounter with God, one cannot fulfill the greatest commandment of loving God or their brother/sister. A pattern will not satisfy one's thirst for living water, leaving

---

255. Daniel Wallace, *Who's Afraid*, 7, as cited in McKnight, Open to the Spirit, 56.

256. Laird R. Harris, Gleason L. Archer, Jr, and Bruce K. Waltke, *Theological Wordbook of the Old Testament*, (Chicago: Moody, 1980), Vol. 1, 366.

an unquenched appetite for more of God. Contemporary spiritual formation literature can further inform biblical ways to fill this longing, and God's reach beyond the Spirit in the text can be further understood through concepts contained in the Hebrew and Greek meanings of *Yada'/ Ginosko,* which I shall also explore.

Learning from contemporary spiritual formation literature

When one's hermeneutic becomes dogmatic, they quit exploring further truth or understanding, because they feel their understanding is right and needs little, if any, further input. The RM can gain much wisdom and insight from others outside of their fellowship, yet has failed to eagerly learn from or often acknowledge their contributions to Christendom. Historical (and contemporary) teachers of spiritual formation outside of the RM have for centuries focused on sustained Christian living from the inside out, beginning with the heart. Their contributions can further inform the RM's interpretive lens and resulting formation.

Anglican bishop and New Testament scholar N.T. Wright captures this reality, "If you want to celebrate—and why not?—then you know what to do. Let the Spirit fill your hearts and lives, particularly your minds and imaginations. Use all the resources of the rich Christian traditions—its poems, its pictures, its liturgies, its hymns—to help you do so."[257] Recently, interest in spiritual formation has caused Protestants and Evangelicals to borrow spiritual rhythms such as meditation, *Lectio Divina,* imaginative prayers, common prayers, and pilgrimages.

Theologian and priest Ron Rolheiser, though from a different religious stream than Keener, adds a similar understanding of Spirit hermeneutics as he teaches that Scripture is not the only way God speaks, as His Holy Spirit is always speaking. He defines other privileged (non-narrative) voices we listen to as the voice of the professional theologian; the voice of piety and various enthusiastic moments; the voice of the poor; and the voice of artists. He believes that the Spirit speaks through them.[258]

---

257. Tom Wright, *Paul for Everyone: The Prison Letters: Ephesians, Philippians, Colossians, and Philemon 2nd ed.* (Louisville, KY: Westminster John Knox, 2004), 64.

258. Ron Rolsheiser, "Teaching and Spirituality," *Teleios* Journal, Vol 1 (2021): 5.

While practices that Wright mentions and non-narrative voices noted by Rolheiser can more robustly feed spiritual formation, these have not been incorporated into the RM churches or ICOC, largely because of the focus on rational thought so entwined in patternism. Belief has included teachings on faith, but has primarily focused on doctrinal belief and Christian actions. According to Marcus Borg, an Anglican, the Latin word *credo* which we translate as "I believe," originally meant "I give my heart to." What/who you give your heart to reveals more of who you are than what you profess to believe or practice.[259] One cannot truly believe without their heart's full engagement with the Lord. The interpretive lens of the Restoration Movement must be intentional in integrating the heart, mind, soul, and strength. This must include a biblical understanding of relational and experiential discipleship. Patternists must add new lenses of dimension to gain such experience.

Adding the relational, experiential dimension to interpretation – Yada'/ Ginosko
     To better understand the added hermeneutical dimension needed for deeper spiritual formation we shall look to the Hebrew understanding of relationship. *Yada'* in Hebrew denotes a knowledge of God gained through relational experience and the senses.[260] In the Greek language, *ginosko* emphasizes the same.[261] This concept invites transformation to a dimension beyond the rational and pragmatic, contrasting the pattern hermeneutic. Dr. Glenn Giles, in studying the 947 occurrences of *yada'* in the Old Testament, notes that most refer to "knowledge gained through the *experience* of life whether *relationally* acquired by *interaction* with other persons or interaction with one's environment.[262]

259. Marcus Borg, *The Heart of Christianity* (NY: Harper Collins,2003), 39-40.

260. Francis Brown, S. R. Driver, and C. A. A. Briggs, *A Hebrew and English Lexicon of the Old Testament*, (Oxford: Clarendon, 1976), 393-94.

261. In the Greek Old Testament (LXX), *ginosko* emphasizes the same.

262. Glenn Giles, "Intimate, Positive, Experiential, Relationship as the Focal Point or Organizational Center and Impetus for the Bible sustained by *Yada'/Ginosko* Theology: An Inquiry." a paper presented at the ICOC Teachers Conference on The Art of Scripture Reading, Feb 25, 2022, 20.

Giles suggests that *Yada'/ginosko* as a theological center informs the disciple that becoming like Christ requires more than doctrinal belief and practice. Relationship is foundational, and should be inseparable from the two. Thus, a pattern hermeneutic is insufficient for relationship with Christ. Throughout the Bible, God makes clear his desire for a heart-to-heart relationship. His desire to be known climaxed with the incarnation of Christ. God also allows Himself to be known, as described in Jn 10:14-15. "I know my sheep and my sheep know me—just as the Father knows me and I know the Father." Jeremiah 31:34 prophesies about the New Covenant: "No longer will a man teach his neighbor, or a man his brother, saying 'Know (*yada'*) the Lord,' because they will all know (*yada'*) me, from the least of them to the greatest, declares the Lord." Jeremiah further prophesies that knowing the Lord is a result of His forgiving and forgetting their sins, thus experiencing His grace.

Giles concludes that to be known by God, one must offer a soft heart of love and obedience. For one to know God, they must desire to experience and receive his goodness, righteousness, justice, loving-kindness, compassion, and faithfulness. *Yada'/ginosko* would also transform relationships between humans where authority is involved (such as governing authorities, church leaders, and in Ancient Middle Eastern culture the slave/master issue) so that in relationships one willingly offers themselves for the good of another out of love and kindness.[263] This transformative way of treating one another models Jesus laying down His life, as described in the well-known hymn in Philippians 2.

As Christians relate on a peer level, transformation happens as they follow the biblical "one another" scriptures that instruct them how to treat each other.[264] However, instruction is not enough without heart transformation that comes from the Spirit. Knowledge and practice without relationship feels forced and insufficient. When relationship becomes the theological center for the biblical message, spiritual formation flows from the

263. Giles, 26.

264. Lanelle Waters, ed, *The One Another Way* (Gainesville, FL: Crossroads Publications, 1979). This is a compilation of scriptures describing God's instructions concerning relationships in the church.

relationship. With this relational focus, one can then form their life priorities and respond to situations in their personal life or in the church. Serving as the foundation for knowledge and practice, the added anaglyph lens can guide the RM's evangelistic Bible teachings of belief, confession, repentance, baptism, and the Holy Spirit alongside the relational and intimate experience with God. They cannot be separated. This relational focus breeds a more fertile ground toward unity, rather than conflicts over different interpretations of *knowing* and *doing*.

Philip Yancey, after his conversation with Henri Nouwen, illustrates this relational imperative.

> Early on, as he sat beside that helpless, child-man [Nouwen was caring for a severely handicapped man, Adam], he realized how marked with rivalry and competition, how obsessive, was his drive for success in academia and Christian ministry. Adam taught him that 'what makes us human is not our mind but our heart, not our ability to think but our ability to love.'[265]

The Spirit takes us beyond the ability to think, transforming our hearts to be filled with the love of Christ. To be spiritually formed in love, patternists must learn to let truth and experience lie together.

Linking Truth and Experience

Recently, a RM professor gave his hermeneutics class the assignment to read a Walt Whitman poem, the Michigan drivers' handbook, a Star Wars quote, and a letter from Emily Dickinson.[266] The students knew that these were different types of literature, but they assumed that only the Michigan drivers' handbook spoke about truth. In their minds, truth was not to be found in poetry, or heart-felt relational dialogue. Such can be the tendency for those raised in the pragmatic, objective RM's patternistic hermeneutical approach. While the professor's classroom assignment can illustrate a general human tendency, the tendency to equate

265. Philip Yancey, *The Jesus I Never Knew*, 120.

266. Shared by Dr. Trevor Cochell in "The Scripture as Story" at "The Art of Scripture Reading," ICOC Teachers Conference, Feb 26, 2022.

truth with rules is exacerbated with a pattern hermeneutic.
Gordon Fee describes the necessary link between exegesis
(an important and necessary part of rational interpretation) and
experience as he insists, "Theology that does not begin and end in
worship is not biblical at all, but is rather the product of western
philosophy. In the same way, I want to insist that the ultimate aim
of all true exegesis is spirituality, in some form or another."[267] Exegesis without the Spirit of God cannot begin or end in worship.

Exegesis can default to a western, rational exercise rather
than its true aim of producing spirituality.[268] Exegesis in conjunc-
tion with the working of the Spirit of God produces fellowship
with God in keeping with His own purposes in the world. Thus,
"'Spirituality' must precede exegesis as well as flow from it."[269] Spiritual exegesis engages the author's Spirituality into the text, not
just their words. This merges the exegete's task beyond analysis
and into the heart of the Spirit of God through the writers. Spiritual exegesis must combine the importance of the author's intended
meaning with the task of Spiritual hearing in such a way that leads
the reader or hearer to worship, to connect with the heart of God,
and to become increasingly transformed into His image. Spiritual interpretation combines knowing, doing, and being so that one
can experience the love of Christ. Paul's prayer for the Ephesians
tells the importance of *experiencing* the love of Christ.

> And may you have the power to understand, as all God's people should, how
> wide, how long, how high, and how deep his love is.
> **May you experience the love of Christ,** though it is too great to understand
> fully. Then you will be made complete with all the fullness of life and power that
> comes from God. Ephesians 3:18-19 NLT (emphasis added)

Patternists must adjust their hermeneutic to engage the
Spirit of God as the transforming, experiential agent it is. Without
such adjustment, one is left with a hermeneutic based on rational
understanding and expectation for ecclesial perfectionism, hardly

267. Gordon Fee, *Listening to the Spirit in the Text* (Grand Rapids, MI: Eerdmans, 2000), 5.
268. Fee uses upper case to emphasize the necessity of the God's Spirit in Spirituality.
269. Fee, *Listening*, 6.

a relational, restful, and sustaining invitation that echoes Jesus' call to take His yoke and learn from Him, finding rest for the soul.

Relationship, Rest, and Receiving in Interpretation

So how does a rational, pragmatic *knower* and *doer* of RM heritage add the relational being to their understanding of spiritual transformation? How does one who holds a one (or two, if we include *knowing* and *doing*) dimensional pattern hermeneutic make room for the Spirit of God? The Psalmist writes, "Be still and know that I am God" (Ps 46:10). God took Sabbath rest, and called His people to "be still." Solitude and stillness allow one to make space to hear and/or experience God to develop an experiential relationship. As Koyama Kosuke notes in *Three Mile an Hour God*, sometimes one must slow down to keep up with God.[270] To go beyond the confines of patternism and learn to receive from God, it becomes necessary to view a more biblical understanding of time and to return to the relational meanings of *yada'/ginosko.*

In the Western mindset, time translates as *chronos* (chronological). When one converts time from *chronos* to *kairos* (right time, the real moment), this brings opportunity for a change of heart. Henri Nouwen recounts that in Jesus' life, every event is recognized as *kairos* (The time has come as in Mk 1:15; the time is near as in Mk 26:10). Jesus changes the *chronos* of human history to *kairos*—God's time, where past, present, and future merge into our present moments.[271] When we view time as *kairos*, every event can lead to a change of heart.

Rethinking Views of Time

Rabbi Abraham Joshua Heschel understands the Jewish connection with holiness and time. While some religions build physical cathedrals, for Jews, Sabbath is "an architecture of time."[272] He explains that spiritual life is not acquiring knowledge but experiencing sacred moments.[273]

---

270. Koyama Kosuke. *Three Mile an Hour God.* London, UK: SCM Press, 2021.

271. Henri Nouwen, *Spiritual Formation* (NY: Harper One, 2010), 8-9.

272. Abraham Joshua Heschel, *The Sabbath* (USA: Farrar, Straus, and Giroux, 1951), xiii.

273. Heschel, *Sabbath*, 6.

Before beginning ministries, many biblical leaders spent time in the wilderness or in the desert. There, they wrestled with and/or experienced God...before they ever began their doing.[274] Jesus went into the wilderness for forty days before beginning his ministry. Paul, after his conversion on the Damascus Road, did not begin his powerful mission to the Gentiles until after he had spent three years in the desert.

Theologian Thomas Merton describes the relationship between time and experiencing God:

> We were indoctrinated so much into means and ends that we don't realize that there is a different dimension.... In technology you have this horizontal progress, where you must start at one point and move to another, and then another...We already have everything, but we don't know it and we don't experience it. Everything has been given to us in Christ. All we need is to experience what we already possess. The trouble is we aren't taking the time to do so.[275]

Without stillness, one cannot consider lilies of the field (Mt 6:28) or compare God's love to sheep beside green pastures and still waters, as David did while out in the fields (Ps 23). Jesus often said, "Hearing they do not hear, seeing they do not see."[276] He calls His hearers to take the needed time to see, hear, and experience God. God has something to give His children. RM interpretation must add the 3D lenses to understand what the lilies of the field and the still waters reveal.

Yada'/ginosko and receiving from God

Patternism highlights *knowing* and *doing*. While knowing and doing draw a person to information about God and ways one can put that information into practice, a relationship goes both ways. Relationship not only involves knowing about God and doing for Him, but it requires the ability to hear and receive from God. How might one interpret scripture to receive from God? For RM inter-

---

274. Consider Noah spent who spent 40 days in an Ark, Moses (Ex 24:18) in the wilderness, Elijah (1 Kings 19:8), and Hagar in the desert where she experiences God (Gen 16).

275. Basil Pennington, *Centering Prayer* (NY: Image, 1980), 56. Cited by Judith Hougen, *Transformed into Fire* (Grand Rapids, MI: Kregel Publishers, 2002), 119.

276. Mt 13:13; Mk 4:12, 8:18.

preters who seek to master Scripture, receiving from Scripture can be neglected, thought to be of little benefit, or even heretical.

Julie Hougen addresses the dilemma of reading without relationship. "We don't read the Bible to simply soak in the Word, but read for the trophy of luminous insights or to plow through so many chapters. We don't want the holy life the disciplines lead us to so much as we want a life wherein we feel wise, useful, and entirely put together." [277]

Without "soaking in the Word," one is left with a hunger and thirsting for more of God. Rational knowledge and practice cannot bring the full expression of God. Receiving while reading and interpreting scriptures allows one to see themselves as the object of God's love and creation. When one hears and reads to receive the living water and to *partake* of the bread that fills the soul, contentment follows. This involves more than theological understanding. Receiving is a heart experience initiated by the Spirit. As one allows the Shepherd who knows His beloved to hold them close to His heart, they become more confident in His love and can give from their overflow.

Receiving from God can be a difficult posture to embrace, especially when one did not experience "being beloved" in their home. This lacking makes it more difficult to accept and be *God's beloved* rather than thinking *we are what we do, what we have, or are what others think of us.*[278] This posture cannot be obtained through a pattern hermeneutic, thus directly affects the patternists' spiritual formation.

In the RM hermeneutic, where one tends to start with what one needs to do, and the correct way to follow a pattern, one rarely begins with *receiving* love. Many devoted Christians have little knowledge of how to experience the love of God. When one has been raised with a pragmatic, rational, and sometimes dogmatic way of interpreting, this becomes even more difficult. In response, the tendency becomes, *I need to be more loving, more vulnerable, more evangelistic and work harder* to experience God more fully. The problem becomes that one then looks to themselves to add,

277. Judith Hougen, *Transformed into Fire* (Grand Rapids, MI: Kregel Publishers, 2002), 158.

278. Henri Nouwen with Michael Christensen and Rebecca Laird, *Discernment: Reading the Signs of Daily Life* (New York: HarperOne, 2013). These thoughts were gathered from Henri Nouwen in *Spiritual Discernment*.

rather than approaching the challenge with complete humility, vulnerability, and dependence on the Spirit's resources. Without such, transformation of the heart becomes unlikely. The pattern hermeneutic must expand from the head to the heart.

From Head to Heart: Unflattening the Pattern

The challenge in growing our hermeneutic beyond the pattern becomes finding the balance between the mind and the heart. Both are essential, but a hermeneutic of the heart requires an ability to form concepts and images about things not physically present. Knowing and doing cannot reach into the longing for experiencing God. C.S. Lewis describes the longing as a "desire for a far-off country...the scent of a flower we have not found, the echo of a tune we have not heard, news from a country we have never yet visited."[279] These thoughts can seem foreign to one who holds a pattern hermeneutic, which is why they must be discussed. Without this connection, lasting spiritual formation cannot take place. Our God-given senses can help awaken these connections.

God created our senses for experience, thus a connection with a relationship with God and our senses becomes vital. These connections can be difficult for one whose hermeneutic seldom ranges beyond the rational, but without them spiritual formation remains something to know about rather than something to experience in increasing measure.

Judith Hougen, in *Transformed into Fire*, describes the difference in head-centered and heart-centered approaches:[280] While we need both, the RM hermeneutic makes the heart-centered focus more challenging; yet, without it we cannot be formed into the image of Christ.

When someone loses a loved one, they generally do not miss facts about them. They grieve the loss of their smile, the look in their eyes, the sound of their voice, their smell, and their touch. While Christians can know the Bible and all its patterns, and even do right actions, one cannot experience God without the Spirit. The Spirit awakens our senses to God.

---

279. C.S. Lewis, *The Weight of Glory* (New York: Harper One, 1976) 31 as cited in Os Guinness, *The Call* (Nashville, TN: W. Publishing, 2003), 16.

280. Hougen, *Transformed*, 36.

Head Centered	Heart Centered
Receives God through intellect	Receives God through imagination
Knowing contained in ideas/concepts	Knowing through experience/emotion
Grounded in willingness to do	Grounded in willingness to be
Responds to God-gives, speaks, initiates	Receives, listens, rests

God wants to fill our senses, which requires a hermeneutic of the heart. Oswald Sanders offers thoughts concerning experiences beyond the rational. "The starvation of the imagination is one of the most fruitful sources of exhaustion and sapping in a worker's life. If you have not used your imagination to put yourself before God, begin to do it now. Imagination is the greatest gift God has given us and it ought to be devoted entirely to Him."[281] For some patternists, these words can feel foreign and even heretical. This is another reason why the pattern hermeneutic must be revised and expanded. God knows we need more.

Experience and sustaining relationship

When reading through the Bible, one discovers that God knows humans need more than information found from words on the page. He uses images, poetry, and symbols to help us understand Him better. In the Old Testament one finds bells, ebenezers, stones of remembrance, marches, festivals, lightings, incense, and so much more. The Bible is full of symbols and metaphors. One cannot fully understand God without metaphors such as the good shepherd, the bread of life, and living water. God reasons with his people through images, metaphors, and paradox. While one can intellectually understand that God loves all people, only the heart can imaginatively receive the love of God spoken to their heart. Patternism does not include such an experiential aspect of interpretation, one that cannot be fully defined and measured.

The Roman-Hellenistic world treasured icons. The art, architecture, coinage, and sculptures sought to convey for the people of that culture the spiritual, unseen realms thought to form the

---

281. Oswald Sanders, *My Utmost for His Highest* (New York: Dodd, Mead, 1935), 42.

context for purpose in life. For example, the church is described as a bride, body, city, temple, stone, building, vineyard, house, kingdom, nation, family, flock, God's people, army, sons of light, salt, leaven, firstborn, priest, and servant. None of these can be reduced to information or objective, qualifying definitions or patterns. Mulholland describes these as channels of thought rather than receptacles of ideas with fixed meanings.[282] 1 Cor 2:13 points to iconography as a major dynamic of scripture. We become participants in God's *kairotic* (beautiful, persuasive, partially subjective) existence.[283] The pattern hermeneutic, resisting that which cannot be rationally obtained from the pages of the text, resists the spiritual formation made possible from "seeing" beyond the information in the text.

James Bryan Smith, in *The Good and Beautiful God*, implores readers to see God by thinking of Him as a great artist and themselves as the art student, noticing carefully every detail of the artist's work.[284] "Seeing" God transforms one's perspective, as studies show.

Studies done with astronauts after returning to earth report a paradigm shift in their thinking. Author Jonah Paquette, after studying the impact of awe, shares words from Edgar Mitchell, Apollo 14 astronaut. "Something happens to you out there. You develop an instant global consciousness, a people orientation, an intense dissatisfaction with the state of the world, and a compulsion to do something about it." Paquette adds:

> For many astronauts, this other dimensional experience beyond their contextual comprehension is so transformative that researchers study it. They find that experiences of awe bring a sense of connectedness to others, that we are more than just ourselves. This often brings greater social connection, more kindness and generosity, and greater curiosity. It orients one toward what matters most in life. Benefits include happiness, less materialistic, more humility, and greater desire to grow and change.[285]

---

282. Robert Mulholland, *Shaped by the Word* (Nashville, TN: Upper Room, 2000) 68-69.

283. Mulholland, *Shaped*, 69.

284. James Bryan Smith, *The Good and Beautiful God: Falling in Love With the God Jesus Knows* (Westmont, IL: Intervarsity Press, 2009), 54.

285. Jonah Paquette, *Awestruck: How Embracing Wonder Can Make You Happier, Healthier, and More Connected* (Boulder, CO: Shambhala), 9-10.

These studies only confirm God's truths. Experiences beyond human rational thought change people, showing them they are part of something much bigger than themselves. These truths cannot be contained by a blueprint. The Spirit uses our senses to help us experience God more fully. A pattern lens cannot adequately involve one's senses, however helpful they may be when interpreting the Bible. Augustine noted the importance of senses as he wrote, "You called, you cried out, you shattered my deafness: you flashed, you shone, you scattered my blindness: you breathed perfume, and I drew in my breath and I pant for you: I tasted, and I am hungry and thirsty: you touched me, and I burned for your peace.[286] This imagery deepens the relational aspect of God and humanity, and explores a dimension unavailable within the pattern.

Spiritual reading is a reading that not only seeks to interpret the scriptures, but also allows the Word to read and interpret one's heart, to hear God. Henri Nouwen suggests, "The Bible is not primarily a book of information about God, but of formation of the heart. It is not merely a book to be analyzed, scrutinized, and discussed, but a book to nurture, unify, and serve as a constant source of contemplation."[287]

Thomas Olbricht spoke of his training in informational or pattern hermeneutics. He first got a glimpse into the possibility of experiencing God in a deeper way through a brother who introduced him to feeling the love of God through meditation and music. The music was to lift him into the presence of God, with genuine spiritual depth. This was uncommon, if not unheard of in the churches of Christ at this time.[288] Incorporating lenses that go beyond rational thought can feel disorienting to patternists. Tim Soerens describes this disorienting phenomenon:

It sounds so simple to learn to pay attention to how the Spirit is working in my life and neighborhood. But the truth is that few of us have been taught to make this our default position. In fact, it might just be the single greatest challenge

286. Augustine, "Confessions," 2001: 229.
287. Henri Nouwen with Michael Christensen and Rebecca Laird, *Spiritual Direction* (NY: Harper One, 2006), 93.
288. Thomas Olbricht, *Hearing God's Voice: My Life with Scripture in the Churches of Christ* (Abilene, TX: ACU Press, 1996), 98.

we have as Christians living in a post-Christian culture. We live and breathe in a culture that has roundly rejected the idea of God's agency in our everyday life. We have moved beyond it as we've moved beyond the horse and carriage. The ideas that God is real—and good—and still active are concepts we have essentially rejected in or everyday lives. But as Charles Taylor notes, we are still haunted by the sacred."[289]

The Scriptures are replete with references about experiencing God beyond rational interpretation, illustrated by passages from both the Old and New Testaments.

"Don't be afraid," the prophet answered. "Those who are with us are more than those who are with them."
And Elisha prayed, "Open his eyes, LORD, so that he may see." Then the LORD opened the servant's eyes, and he looked and saw the hills full of horses and chariots of fire all around Elisha. (2 Kings 6:16-17)

I keep asking that the God of our Lord Jesus Christ, the glorious Father, may give you the Spirit of wisdom and revelation, so that you may know him better.
I pray that the eyes of your heart may be enlightened in order that you may know the hope to which he has called you, the riches of his glorious inheritance in his holy people, and his incomparably great power for us who believe. (Eph 1:17-19)

The psalter contains myriad references to that which one beholds beyond the physical. Artists, musicians, and poets help one develop the "third eye" that sees another dimension such as expressed by poet Elizabeth Barrett Browning.

Earth's crammed with heaven,
And every common bush afire with God;
But only he who sees takes off his shoes;
The rest sit round it and pluck blackberries.[290]

---

289. Soerens, *Everywhere You Look*, 38, quoting Charles Taylor, *A Secular Age* (Cambridge, MA: Belknap Press), 2007, 593.

290. Elizabeth Barrett Browning, *Aurora Leigh* (NY: C.S. Francis, 1857), 276.

As one adjusts their hermeneutic to better experience God, His holiness becomes more evident, thus providing more sustainable spiritual formation.

Conclusion

The role of God's Spirit, viewed in varied ways throughout Restoration Movement history, plays a profound role in a Christian's formation into the image of Christ. A one (or two) dimensional hermeneutic can hinder one's relational dynamic with God, stunting or fossilizing their spiritual growth and leaving them with a desire for more. Since the beginning of time, God has sought a relationship with humankind, as understood from His continual desire for *yada'/ginosko*. While rational interpretation cannot be neglected, it is inadequate for exploring and experiencing the depths of God. Encounters through the Word, the Spirit, nature, one's senses, and intentional integration of a multi-dimensional Spirit lens helps develop, deepen, strengthen, and sustain one's lifelong spiritual formation. Those who employ a pattern hermeneutic develop "head centered," rational interpretive methods, but the "heart centered" dimension often remains underdeveloped.

Orthodoxy (knowing) and orthopraxis (doing) remain essential components of Christian faith. However, with the neglect of orthocardia (the heart), Christian faith stalls, remaining incomplete and unsustainable. As noted in the greatest commandment (Mt 22:37-40), the heart relationship must be integrated with the mind, soul, and strength.

Reason and experience are not incompatible and must be intentionally integrated within the RM hermeneutic. This will require humility, a faith that allows uncertainty, belief that God is beyond human understanding, and time that allows space for God to transform from within. Faith includes rational interpretation and discipleship, but must not negate or neglect the intimate, experiential role (being) that the Bible includes. God intends this intimate relationship to be both personal and communal. Keener notes, "Ideally the entire church must be experiential if it wishes to be biblical."[291]

---

291. Keener, *Spirit Hermeneutics*, 11.

By integrating the "anaglyph" lens of the Spirit in Bible interpretation, members can experience deeper, more sustainable transformation. Though this multi-dimensional Spirit lens can be feared by the rational patternist who seeks to master the Word, it can open the eyes of one's heart, forming their experience through the hope, power, and glorious inheritance that comes from God (Eph 1:18-19).

292

292. Image by Dave Blazek, used with permission.

CHAPTER FIVE

Conclusion:
Reimagining an Integrated,
Unity-Producing,
Spirit-Formed Hermeneutic

Unity is achieved when we see the *imago Dei* in one another, when we refuse to
live by the cultural script that some lives have more value than others. Unity thus
honors diversity. Unity requires vigilant curiosity, a common story, and the kind of
humility that most of us (myself included) do not value... The call for uniformity is
a classic of the majority with deep roots in the logic of colonization. It's a dangerous
substitute to the unity we are commanded to work toward.[293]

God exhibits perfect unity as three in one, and Jesus' last
prayer, recorded in John 17, was a desperate plea for unity among
Christians to mirror the unity of the Triune God. Spiritual formation begets unity, as one's formation into the image of Christ
leads to this relational togetherness. As my lens examination has
journeyed through the history of the pattern hermeneutic in the
Restoration Movement (and its effect on spiritual formation), explored continuing implications for formation, introduced clarifying lenses needed for more robust transformation, and demonstrated the need for a deeper understanding and experience of the
Spirit a question remains: Will patternism allow the noble goal of
unity, called for by the Movement founders? To answer this question, I shall recount early RM leaders' pleas for unity and show
reasons why patternism hinders this noble goal from its inception
until now. I next explore several current ICOC teachers' views on
patternism and unity, and lastly, I offer suggestions for teachings
and habits toward building greater unity amid diversity in the
church today as she, in humility, depends on the Spirit of God to
lead her.

---

293. Soerens, *Everywhere You Look*, 88.

Unity and Diversity: Back to the Future

Barton Stone, in many of his final published messages, pleaded for ministers to return to brotherly love. He felt that those who were argumentative and unrelenting on their sectarian views should spend more time in devotion to God. He believed that worship, as one drew close to the throne of God, would create humility and other Christlike attitudes. He knew that the Spirit remained essential for unity, as human attempts are vain. He compared unity without the Spirit to tying bundles of sticks together, hoping they would bear fruit. First, each branch must be united to its living source, receive its sap and Spirit, and only then can be united to each other.[294] He was reluctant to enforce any kind of pattern on other believers or use it as a test of fellowship.

In 1835 he wrote:

> The scriptures [sic] will never keep together in union, and fellowship members not in the spirit of the scriptures, which spirit is love, peace, unity, forbearance, and cheerful obedience. This is the spirit of the great Head of the body. I blush for my fellows, who hold up the Bible as the bond of union yet make their opinions of it tests of fellowship; who plead for union of all christians; yet refuse fellowship with such as dissent from their notions.[295]

In his "Address to the Churches" he taught, "One thing I have ever observed, that in every revival of pure religion, the spirit of tolerance revives with it; and as [pure religion] declines, intolerance increases. Pure religion expands the souls of Christians; but bigotry contradicts them."[296]

At one time both Campbell and Stone considered the fruit of the Spirit in one's life more telling of one's Christianity than adherence to doctrine, but somewhere along the way the original plea of the RM moved from desire for unity to a need to find a pattern for first-century New Testament Christianity. The two do not mix well. Perhaps Campbell's approach was distorted, even if his original intent was not.

294. Barton W. Stone, "The Retrospect," Christian Messenger 7 (October 1833): 316.

295. Barton Stone, "Remarks," *Christian Messenger,* August 1835, 180.

296. Barton Stone, "Address to the Churches," in *The Works of Elder B.W.Stone,* 157.

Campbell's approach (both Thomas and Alexander) became more influential because the church seemed to value structure and certainty over Stone's loose commitment to freedom and unity. The influence of the Enlightenment, the Age of Reason, and the scientific method took precedence. One cannot help but wonder, if Stone's pen had been as active as Campbell's, and if he had lived longer, if the movement might have been known as a unity movement more than a restoration movement. A RM leader of the late 1800s and early 1900s, T. B. Larrimore, imagined a unity far from what we observe throughout RM history:

Indeed, I believe extremists, hobbies and hobbyists are cursing the cause of Christ to-day beyond the comprehension of mortal man. And, unfortunately, some sincere souls seem to be determined to never recognize as Christians, or have fellowship with any, save those who ride their hobby. Let me walk forever rather than ride a religious hobby; and let me die today rather than be deprived of my Christian liberty. 'The perfect law of liberty' is not 'the yoke of bondage,' nor is it a law of slavery...

It is never safe to assume that a certain passage of sacred scripture means a certain thing, when it may mean something else and not mean what it is assumed to mean at all, and reasoning from that assumption may be false; and consequently, our conclusion may not only be erroneous, but even dangerous and harmful...

But I shall not do that. I do not, shall not and should not assume to be wiser, worthier or better than my brethren; but it is ever safe for any and all of us to investigate, always being open to conviction and appreciating instruction and correction.[297]

The original plea for unity from the early Restoration Movement leaders soon became blurred, as the search for the pattern resulted in legalistic and judgmental postures. Human, sinful nature surely played a part, but a hermeneutic that failed to incorporate a focus on the narrative of the biblical story, the redemptive movement of God, and the Holy Spirit contributed to what became an understanding of Scripture that hindered spiritual transformation

297. "Fellowship," Letters and Sermons of T. B. Larimore, vol 3, edited by Emma Page (Nashville, TN: McQuiddy Printing, 1910), 184-188.

and encouraged division.

Jack Reese, after offering a poignant reminder of the noble beginning of the RM and a time when extraordinary unity was practiced, followed with the realization that unity was challenged when the interpretation of the biblical pattern differed. The expression "unity in diversity" to many church leaders threatened the Movement's reasons for existing and seemed contradictory. They assumed their "back to the Bible" pattern hermeneutic would unite everyone in all truth without disagreement. He explains that unity makes no sense without diversity or differences in opinion. He believes that if we are united only when in agreement it:

> ...denies the power of the cross and the witness of the church... Loving each other in the midst of differences cuts against the grain of the world because it stands in stark contrast with what the world considers normal. Anyone can be united with friends when they all agree. It takes a different kind of love to be united with people with whom we acutely disagree. But that's what unity is. And it is precisely what Jesus calls us to do.[298]

He concludes with the realization that as the church forgot the pleas of the founding fathers, the way things were done became systematized and set as rules that became gospel, replacing the true Gospel. He tells his readers, "We can observe a lot by watching."[299] The only way the RM, including the ICOC, can observe and watch is by understanding their past history and hermeneutic.

Reese looks back as he looks forward, asking penetrating questions while offering a thoughtful charge toward gentleness and humility for all whose history traces through the Restoration Movement:

> Would they be able to discern the echoes of their past, already grown faint? Would they recall the memories of a time when the unity of all Christians was the primary concern of this people? Would they remember to be gentle? Would they remember to listen?...

---

298. Reese, *The Blue Hole*, 160.
299. Reese, *The Blue Hole*, 196.

The meanings we construct from the patterns we see are only partial and are notoriously unreliable. That's why humility is so critical. That is why we need other perspectives, more input, different voices to help us see more clearly. [300]

Varied and informed voices must be heard if there is any hope for increased unity inside and outside of our church stream, thus voices of contemporary, recognized teachers from streams within the RM offer such insight into the connection between hermeneutics and the transformation that leads toward either unity or disunity.

Can Unity and Diversity Co-exist in Patternism?

The RM churches, including the ICOC, miss many blessings of unity because of its sectarian posture. Douglas Jacoby notes, "Patternism leads to a lack of respect [for those who interpret differently]. Thus, we don't connect, network, or benefit from the wisdom of others. This is a massive problem."[301] Reese adds to this view, applicable to both the mainstream churches of Christ and the ICOC:

Churches of Christ, however, are facing some particular obstacles. Our longtime isolation from others and the growing polarization within the movement itself have made matters worse. We have historically cut ourselves off from other groups, so we missed what we might have learned in such a dialogue. More than that, we have cut ourselves off from our own story. We are thirsty and don't know why, and we can't seem to figure out who to blame for the drought.[302]

To change this "pattern" in our history, it becomes imperative for the church to discern ways this history continues to affect us today so that we can develop new patterns and habits. History repeated itself as the RM churches continued in sectarian postures. Beginning in the 1980s, the mainstream churches of Christ were looked down upon by the ICOC as lukewarm and uncommitted fellowships. Many of McKean's sermons and writings treated the

---

300. Jack R. Reese, *At The Blue Hole:Elegy for a Church on the Edge* (Grand Rapids, MI: Eerdmans, 2021) 103, 105.

301. Interview with Douglas Jacoby.

302. Reese, *The Blue Hole*, 41.

mainstream church of Christ with suspicion and disdain. Even the ICOC's public sharing of "good news among the churches" encouraged sectarian views in subtle ways. News sharing venues brought encouragement and faith, but also contributed to underlying sectarian views. Through McKean's persuasive and oft-inspiring rhetoric, stories were told in ways that insinuated that God's Modern-Day Movement (the ICOC) uniquely facilitated acts of God. Apartheid ended because of *our* church's faith to plant a biracial church in South Africa; the Berlin wall fell after *we* planted a church in Berlin; the Iron Curtain fell because *we* planted a church in Russia.[303] God seemed to follow the ICOC movement.

Although God worked in astounding ways within the ICOC in response to the faith of men and women who went to the mission field, no acknowledgement or honor was bestowed on men and women of other Christian groups who had given their lives for years—sometimes literally—for these causes. The exclusive posture suggested that very few outside of the ICOC were true Christians, as the ICOC had the "most correct" understanding of life and doctrine. Within the mainstream churches of Christ and the ICOC, members were referred to by both others and themselves as "a people of the book." Kinder confirms, "In many circles they are known for being a people of the book—for quoting Scripture frequently in their messages.... They were also known in many sectors for a rugged exclusivism."[304] Perhaps instead of being known as "people of the book," it would be more transforming to carry the description "people of Jesus." While the "book" should lead to Jesus, too often the ways one interprets the "book" bring separation and the deforming postures previously discussed.

Among the six ICOC teachers I interviewed, only one had a hope for unity within our churches or among other RM churches as long as we continue to hold to our deeply rooted pattern hermeneutic. David Pocta held hope that "if it's framed right, and we understand the role that patternism should play and limit it to its role, it can be helpful." He added:

> As I step out of our world and talk about Catholicism, the value of a monastic

---

303. *Visions and Dreams,* "Disciples Today," 2010. https://youtu.be/rJeps7C6VYI.

304. Kinder, Donald M., *Capturing Head and Heart: The Lives of Early Popular Stone-Campbell Movement Leaders* (Abilene, TX: Leafwood Publishers, 2012), 11.

life is that one learns the disciplines and repetition of prayer. I think unity is absolutely possible if we limit the understanding to the role that it [patternism] plays in our spiritual development and then seeing that there's much more to it. There are some really amazing things that have come out of the ICOC. It was built on this idea that we could actually imitate the life of a disciple from the early church, and at its core that's what made us who we are. It was amazing— until it wasn't amazing.[305]

Robert Carrillo, remarking on the role of patternism in transformation and unity shared:

Jesus says that true worshipers worship in spirit and truth. I think we like the truth part and assume everyone will recognize the truth. I think we tend to be afraid of the spirit part, which has a huge role in our spiritual development. Spiritual formation is not self-formation. It is born of the Spirit. Ephesians 4 teaches us to keep the unity of the Spirit, not the unity of the doctrine. Unity comes from the Holy Spirit more than from doctrine. Scripture has many forks in the road in interpretation, so if only agreement on Scripture unites us, we will not be united. Jesus left us with more than the Bible. He had to leave so the Spirit could come. Scripture should lead us to God, not a pattern. Jesus did not call us to unity with the first-century church. The Spirit can bring unity.[306]

Carrillo explains that underlying patternism is the desire for certainty, and that desire for certainty is what affects unity. Restoration Movement churches, including the ICOC, have taught the importance of obedience to God, but have also taught—as is the result of a blueprint hermeneutic—that there should be uniformity in the ways we read and follow the Scriptures. Interpretations outside of accepted patterns automatically create separations of fellowship. Patternism demands certainty, which then demands uniformity. With this formula, unity can seldom, if ever, be achieved. This posture assumes we will all read the Bible and come to the exact same conclusions.[307] He adds:

We have difficulty believing and practicing anything not clearly stated in Scripture. This is problematic since there are various teachings that are not clearly

---

305. Interview with David Pocta.

306. Interview on Zoom with Robert Carillo, October 20, 2020.

307. Robert Carrillo interview.

stated or explained. When we encounter ambiguity in a scripture, wisdom and discernment is required from the Holy Spirit. Patternism doesn't leave much room for the Holy Spirit to move, because our view is if it's not recorded in the first century Scriptures then it's subject to suspicion . . . it's almost like we would interrogate or question the Holy Spirit if the Spirit can't show us book, chapter, and verse. Unity of the spirit is as important as unity of doctrine. Our patternistic, literalist hermeneutic requires such uniformity. It leads us to think we are the only ones saved.[308]

When Christians are trained to look for a pattern to obey, to use as the example, or to discern as a necessary inference, history shows there is little hope for unity. Douglas Jacoby speaks of the formative reasons behind patternism which leads to disunity:

It always seems insightful to have a pattern. It brings security to think we have the right way and have discovered the truth. But that then fossilizes; it becomes rigid, very black and white. Patterns can also become boring, because you have been taught all you need to know. I think it leads to disrespect, arrogance, and judgmentalism. We don't connect, network with others outside our tribe, and benefit from the wisdom of others. Also, without biblical training, people can become susceptible to other patterns that involve more political or social interpretations of the Gospel.[309]

While these statements can be discouraging concerning unity, there is hope through spiritual formation. As Christians move closer to Him, they become closer to each other. The Spirit produces unity. To illustrate the current difficulty of navigating unity in diversity I shall use an example in my family of churches from 2020.

A Case Study: When Unity is Assumed but not Discussed, Disunity Results.

Several years ago, the ICOC teachers[310] commissioned a task

---

308. Robert Carrillo interview.

309. Interview with Douglas Jacoby.

310. The ICOC has recognized teachers from different congregations. A geographical subset of these teachers make up a service team meant to serve the ICOC churches. This service team gathered a task force to study the role of women in the church.

force to study the role of women in the church and give their combined findings to the churches. This hard-working group gathered virtually for several hours most Saturday mornings throughout the year as papers were assigned, written, and then discussed. Assignments were given for exegeting scriptures pertaining to the women's role in Genesis 1 and 2, 1 Cor. 11, 1 Cor 14, Galatians 3, 1 Timothy 2, and 1 Peter 3. After completion, they were published as a book and advertised to the ICOC churches.[311] During the process, when it became clear that the task force would not come to full agreement, two in the group asked to discuss how the church will handle unity in diversity. The following request from one of these individuals was given to the group:

> I believe a lack of discussion and exploration of Biblical interpretation affects our churches in many and various ways. Our overall interpretive approach could be described as "selective literalism." Some scriptures on this topic are taken literally even in the same passages where we view others as cultural.
>
> In my experience in the Churches of Christ for the past six decades, I have noted a strong tendency toward the thinking that our church holds the truth and is correct in all doctrine. It's not just a tendency; it has been taught for years. At least this is what I was taught. While I personally do not know of another church that teaches many doctrines closer to the Bible (as I interpret it), this posture can lead us as a church toward lack of eagerness for learning and listening, as well as a temptation toward judgmental attitudes.
>
> While the discussion at hand is focused on the role of women in the church, as we are aware, some leaderships in our individual churches have already been studying this topic and have also come to varied opinions. This comes as no surprise, as Bible scholars have been unable to come to shared conclusions for centuries.
>
> I can't help but wonder if the more pressing, undergirding discussions should be about interpretation and unity. How might we, as a family of churches, love each other and accept one another even if (when) we hold differing views on matters that do not affect one's salvation? Of course, the challenge is that some hold different views about what matters/beliefs/practices do affect one's salvation. Some might hold these views I shall mention as salvation issues;

---

311. The series of exegetical studies was published in 2020 with the title, *The Bible and Gender*. ICOC teachers, The Bible and Gender (Spring, TX: Illumination Publishers), 2020.

some would hold none of these as salvation issues. If something is not a salvation issue, must it be a fellowship issue?

How might we add greater amounts of humility and love into our discussions on differing views? Personally, I believe we can have certain differing views and be united, but as our brother aptly expressed, something quite different will have to change in our overall thinking in order to do this. As many have noted, *this is not in our church culture or DNA*. How might we love each other and practice unity when we disagree? If we focus on such disagreements, we will certainly fail to reach as many as possible with the saving message of Jesus.

Many different views currently exist throughout our fellowship of churches. I have listed "differences" that quickly came to mind. It seems to me each of these views are held because of one's interpretation of Scripture, and prayerfully are all influenced by one's desire to be faithful to Scripture. Nonetheless, they differ. These include matters such as:

- Differing political views. Any cursory reading of Facebook will show that faithful Christians are divided, often sharing strong opinions that could make one think that to hold a differing opinion is non-Christian. Some hold to nationalism for various reasons they think biblical, while others believe nationalism is contrary to the Kingdom of God.

- Different views on pacifism. Some believe that bearing arms is in direct opposition to the teachings of Jesus, while others believe one would be wrong if they did not protect their country or family.

- Differing views of racism; some feel that others are out of touch with reality and hold racist attitudes unknowingly, and others can feel things are fine as they are.

- Differing views/practices on alcohol consumption.

- Different views on dancing (within and outside of worship services).

- Some believe that house churches are the biblical model of corporate worship and others believe a church for every city is biblical.

- Some hold that communion is biblical when shared as a meal, and others are fine with a quick passing of matza bread and grape juice.

- Different views of the scriptural acceptability of corporate worship on Saturday evening (Jewish time) while some hold this is non-biblical.

- Different views of appropriate dress for corporate worship. Some feel casual will help in outreach and others feel "Sunday best" shows honoring of God.

- Differing views and practices concerning leadership teams; one-man leadership; and amounts of control practiced by leaders and members alike.

- Different views/practices of our "study series" used to teach non-Christians how to be saved. (Even in our basic study series, when examining the above hermeneutic approaches, some of the scriptures can easily be used out of context.)

- Different views of modesty and acceptable dress codes.

- Differing views on dating "guidelines" for dating couples and different views on dating "believers" in other churches.

- Differing views on divorce. . . some who believe one who marries after divorce, or marries someone divorced (no matter whether there was adultery, or if it happened before becoming a Christian) is living in adultery, while others believe differently.

- Churches have different views and practices of elder qualifications. Some believe all children must be faithful Christians, and others believe they simply must have a good relationship with their parents. Some believe elders must not have been married before becoming a Christian or even had a spouse who died, while others hold a different view.

- Different views of the creation "days."

- Differing views of hell: eternal fire or a just punishment followed by annihilation.

- Different views on what happens when we die: heaven, paradise, asleep, or other.

- Different views on acceptable styles of worship music.

- Different views of what is acceptable as treating our bodies as a temple of the Spirit. Smoking is unacceptable and yet significant unhealthy eating habits are acceptable.

- Some hold that taking care of God's creation is part of being righteous while others do not hold this as a biblical matter of importance.

- Different views of how one must "be broken" to be ready for baptism and what a person must understand before they are baptized.

- Different views on the role of women. Some allow women to teach in mixed audiences; some don't allow women to share at communion or speak in any way; some insist on a man being on stage with a woman. Some believe a woman may preach a sermon and perform weddings while others believe this is out of place for a woman. Some have women pray in the worship service, while others believe that is an authoritative act, and thus, unbiblical.

- We have traditions and differing views of appointing evangelists, women's ministry leaders, deacons, and deaconesses, and little is mentioned on biblical definitions of evangelists, apostles, prophets, prophetesses, etc.

- Some might think that a discussion like this would be inappropriate, while others believe the healthiest approach, and the one that has us relying on God and continually growing is that one which is honest and totally transparent about the areas where we have differences (and see this as a place for the Spirit to work).

As previously noted, some want a "bottom line" on the discussion of the women's role. This dilemma helps define a problem—that as a church family, it seems we do not yet know well how to disagree or accept varied plausible possibilities of interpretation without judgment. I certainly do not have the answers, but I am sure that love, humility, and acceptance are vital as we move forward.

Does a discussion like this leave us adrift in a sea of uncertainty? Some might think so, but as previously observed, we have God's clear messages of love, humility, holiness, and wholehearted devotion that change the way one lives their life. During my decades in the church, I have seen many practices (once held as sacred) change as we have gained further understanding, as have you. We have personally witnessed wonderful workings of God through the church as well as terribly flawed leadership. But I believe we have also learned that God works in the lives of flawed people when they wrestle honestly with life and truth and keep seeking God's will.

While I personally do not see any of the above issues as "salvation issues" (though some may), some of the differing views are more visible than others; thus, each church leadership has decided or will decide such things as qualifications for elders, what is acceptable and unacceptable for women in their churches, models of corporate worship, and other more visible practices. Perhaps, to help build unity, these leadership decisions could be expressed with acknowledgment that *there are other plausible views that faithful Christians hold,* yet of course each leadership determines specific practices in their churches for reasons they deem best—while not passing judgment on and giving freedom to those who interpret differently. Christians should also take responsibility for doing their study and coming to their own decisions—seeking to promote unity rather than division even if they would like to see something practiced differently.

Perhaps it's too lofty a vision, but I would like to believe that a Christian community's focus on holiness, humility, love for each other and the lost, service, praising and honoring God can bring unity and can overcome our differences—if we let them.[312]

In response to an earlier request for further conversation on unity in diversity, one member of the task force commented:

On the hermeneutical question, I think we also have to be aware of our own history and tendency to want to find a blueprint/pattern that can be applied for all time to all peoples and in all places. I'm not sure that was God's/the author's intention for many of these passages (mostly ad hoc letters), although I recognize that there are clearly some universal principles to be found in some of the passages. Many of the relevant passages we have identified are difficult passages, and I think we have to develop some level of comfort in saying at the end of the day that there are different ways that they can be reasonably interpreted, and allow room for people within our fellowship to hold to these different interpretations in good conscience. Also, I think we must recognize that the different cultures in our worldwide fellowship will defy any attempt to successfully impose a standard approach we seek to discern from Scripture. In essence, I guess I am saying that we are not likely to find one pattern we can commend to all our churches around the world. More likely, we can discern principles and teach those, and perhaps will need to leave the specific application for those principles to individual churches; an approach that would perhaps be new for us as our fellowship tends to prefer certainty and a specific rule/protocol to follow.[313]

Unfortunately, this topic concerning ways to maintain unity in diversity was never put on the agenda or discussed in the group. The group ended with the completion of a paper exegeting

---

312. This was from correspondence within the task force dated August 17, 2019. I was the author.
313. From Courtney Bailey PhD, ICOC teacher, Kingston, Jamaica. Used with permission.

selected passages on the role of women in the church, but without any discussion concerning ways to hold to unity with differing views among churches, or even among the task force.

Patternism's inherent desire for certainty over the years has led to dogmatic stances which bred a mindset that uniformity (in doctrine and practice) was necessary in order to achieve unity.

Thus far, we have not yet learned how to remain united as a family of churches when there are differing church beliefs and/or practices on such things as the role of women, the assembling of house churches, and various other diversities. While a congregation may state that they consider those with different views to be fellow Christians and brothers and sisters in Christ, when they are not included in church locators and/or encouraged for such activities as dating and fellowship, do not our actions state otherwise?

The preceding paragraph is not meant to suggest what potentially could become reality. Real-life examples could be supplied, regrettably. That said, my purpose is not to unnecessarily stir the waters of any existing situation. Rather, my hope is to encourage further discussion aimed at limiting progression toward further separation and hopefully even implement some reversals that would provide increased unity.

Formation into Christlikeness must include unity. In His last recorded prayer before He went to the cross, Jesus prayed for the unity of His followers to be like the unity He and the Father share (Jn 17:20-23). Until the church's hermeneutical "pattern" views salvation and fellowship issues such as the "ones" described in Ephesians 4:4-6 (one Lord, one faith, one baptism, one God and Father of us all...) rather than the oft-disputed patterns, unity without uniformity will prove impossible, as history documents. Patternism stands in the way of unity without uniformity. Disunity breeds judgment and pride, and judgment and pride breed disunity. These postures oppose spiritual formation. Perhaps this is why in the preceding verses Paul states, "Be completely humble and gentle; be patient, bearing with one another in love. Make every effort to keep the unity of the Spirit through the bond of peace" (Eph 4:2-5).

Jesus' prayer for unity deserves full attention, as separation stemming from diversity continues. While patternists believe their view is the way to hold to "sound doctrine" and yet often disagree on what is considered sound, perhaps Jesus would consider unity among believers as "more sound." Christians' formation into the image of Christ remains the hope for unity.

The Spirit Begets Unity

Spiritual formation flows from the Spirit. It may be bound by doctrine and practice, but originates from neither. Doctrine and practice can describe and illustrate unity and mission, but they cannot produce or sustain it. Spiritual formation must include both unity and mission, because transformation into the image of Christ implies a heart of both. Though he was addressing racial unity, Douglas Foster's words apply to all kinds of unity:

> I am convinced that racial healing and unity must begin with the work of spiritual formation together: meditating on scripture and spiritual readings, listening to each other's stories, coming to know the realities of American racism as experienced by our brothers and sisters of color, looking each other in the eyes and repenting of racist attitudes, and kneeling together in prayer.[314]

He noted that unity is never easy and though often opposed in the name of Christianity, it must be the responsibility of Christians. Unity and missional growth started well in the beginning days of the Restoration Movement. Both have since ebbed and flowed, but neither have grown in a sustained upward trajectory.

Mission also begins in spiritual formation. One can know that the mission to seek and save the lost is God's will and can evangelize out of duty, but Jesus' mission flows from the Spirit of God. John Mark Hicks, in attempting to recenter one's thinking writes:

> Reason cannot drive mission; it will burn out...It seems that human rationality often presumes that it can describe or even prescribe the limits of what is possible for God. This rationalistic approach assumes a realist understanding of

314. Douglas A. Foster, "An Essay on Unity," Dec 5, 2020, as cited in https://www.douglasjacoby.com/a-unity-essay-by-douglas-a-foster/.

the attributes of God, one that believes those attributes can be truly known, processed, and delimited by human rationality... Rational understandings of God that constrain God are replaced with the praise of the God who is known through Scripture, experienced in life's situations, and encountered in corporate worship. Instead of rationalistic and metaphysical grids, we seek God in a worship encounter and praise his attributes rather than try to plumb the depths of their logical relations.[315]

Hicks' remarks accentuate the dependence on God's Spirit and a heart focus over human rationality. These two attributes must be demonstrated in relationships with fellow Christians, encountering each other in corporate worship. The pattern hermeneutic influences members' views of community.

Though the patterns and examples of churches in the New Testament would call for unity, as examples have shown, the pattern concerns itself with perceived inferences and examples of ecclesial order in the church, leading to disunity on issues from instruments, mission societies, the women's role, and dozens of other diversified interpretations. To change this tendency, the ability to find unity in diversity must be imagined and employed. This requires serious adjustments to our default hermeneutical lens.

Bobby Valentine poses ways that patternism has hindered unity in the RM churches and reminds that the churches in the New Testament were not carbon copies of each other. He notes that there were serious divisions in the churches then, especially because the churches in Jerusalem, Judea, and Galilee did not do the same things in the same ways that the Gentile churches did, especially those Paul began. Acts 15, Acts 21:17-27, and Acts 24:11-18 confirm this observation. The brothers, amid the diversity, affirmed each other as brothers. Paul and James did not cast disparagement on each other. Both, according to Acts 15:6-29, were right in their differing conclusions concerning circumcision and food sacrificed to idols. He then poses a poignant question. "Could you maintain fellowship with a man who offered animal sacrifices? And, could you maintain fellowship with a church that did the

315. John Mark Hicks, "Recentering," *Teleios,* Vol 1, No 2 (2021): 65.

same?" This is what James, Paul, Luke, and the Jerusalem church did. Paul's example in Acts 20:7 (serving communion every first day of the week) was seen as binding, and yet in Acts 21:17-24 (circumcision, purification rites) and 24:11-18 (adhering to the law), Paul's and James' example was not.[316] Unity in diversity is possible. Perhaps we need to go way back to the future and learn from James, Paul, and Luke. To experience the prayer Jesus prayed for the church, a new vision of unity in diversity, so desired by the early RM leaders, must be re-imagined, intentional, and forged.

Preparing for the Future

In the early 1970s, in my hometown of Gainesville, Florida, two high schools (one black and one white) converged into one, following a court-ordered desegregation. While the court order demanded immediate logistical changes, successful integration did not follow. Lawyer Michael Gengler documented the tumultuous and sometimes violent challenges in his book, *We Can Do It: A Community Takes on the Challenge of School Desegregation.* The author interviewed me concerning my experiences as a student leader during this time and notes, "Not one of the thirty-three former students who agreed to be interviewed understood in February 1970 what had caused the end of Alachua County's dual system in February 1970....They agreed there was little warning or preparation at Lincoln (the all black high school) or Gainesville High (predominantly white)."[317] Students were mostly unaware of deep-rooted racial issues and the grief and loss involved in losing a familiar community. They held presuppositions of the ways things were meant to be, and there were no teachings, conversations, or forums to learn from each other. Similarly, if the RM movement churches, including the ICOC, cannot better understand and teach church history, varied hermeneutical emphases, presuppositions carried into our venues, and the role of the Spirit of God in leading us forward, the churches will not experience integration of differing points of view. Unity cannot be forced, but

---

316. Bobby Valentine, https://www.wineskins.org/articles/2022/01/03/six-things-i-pray-for-churches-of-christ-in-2022?rq=Six%20Things%20I%20pray, Dec 5, 2020.

317. Michael Gengler, *We Can Do It: A Community Takes on the Challenge of School Desegregation* (New York: Rosetta Books, 2018), 368-369.

must be intentionally sought and forged. With this in mind, I offer suggestions for our churches.

Suggestions for Intentional Implementation of Lens Adjustments

While curriculums can be helpful and necessary to fill gaps in our church teachings, I first offer Rubel Shelley's contemporary plea for unity, applicable to every person. Shelley, former Rochester College president and Lipscomb University professor, remains a constant proponent of unity in the RM churches. He offers the following practices to consider, which will take thoughtful discernment to implement. His plea asks members to:

1. Pray for the unity of the church.

2. Repent of any tribal elitism in your own history and heart.

3. Refuse to caricature or make fun of others...this dehumanizes people.

4. Make Jesus the focus...do not argue your position.

5. Look for evidence of God's activity in other people...Why can't I affirm what I see when I see the Spirit at work in others' lives? When others are serving to the best of their ability, affirm it. We have all received grace.

6. Be part of a church that focuses on Jesus because it loves Scripture.

7. Study what the Bible says about love, and reconciliation. Doctrinal soundness is incomplete. Difference is not deviance.

8. Take some baby steps toward unity...it happens at the grass roots....

9. Deep convictions are necessary for unity. Let us not sit in judgment of each other.

10. Don't be bullied by someone else's narrowness.[318]

These considerations could mark the beginnings of a re-envisioned unity. Continual teaching and reminders must be

---

318. This list of ten practices was distributed at "Harbor: The Pepperdine Bible Lectures" from Rubel Shelly, September, 2022. These were also shared on the "Common Grounds Unity Podcast" episodes 66 and 67.

deliberate and on-going. And, since one cannot know their history without learning it or adjust their hermeneutic without awareness of their own and/or other possibilities, I suggest that in our churches we teach both leaders and members basic Restoration Movement history. It is both incomplete and presumptuous to assume our church began at Pentecost and has no founders other than Christ. In the ICOC, many still remember the teachings from the 1980s through the early 2000s that "God's Modern-Day Movement" began in a Boston suburb in Massachusetts in 1979. Such teachings, though not often still taught today, have not been publicly corrected or untaught, so they often remain assumed, resulting in confusion about our history.

While God has worked powerfully through the ICOC members' knowledge of "First Principles" classes that teach about salvation and offer study tools to teach to their family, friends, and even strangers, these teachings should be adjusted to include the big picture teaching of the biblical narrative. Currently, these study series can become set in stone, viewed as dogma to be followed. A basic understanding of how the Bible is written (including genres and cultural literary devices) should also be taught to expand hermeneutical lenses to bring "meat" that follows the young Christian's milk diet (1 Cor 3:2). Simple tools such as comparing the interpretation of scriptures through the four lenses illustrated in chapter 3 would be helpful for expanding one's interpretive instincts. A basic understanding of ways to interpret Scripture will help navigate growth rather than stagnation and promote humility and unity over judgmental, arrogant postures.

Consistent teaching should be offered in spiritual formation, with an emphasis on the Spirit transforming us instead of relying on our own efforts. Classes and workshops on building relational connections to encourage change from the inside out must be taught to members. Churches should consider pulpit swaps, and members can be encouraged to read other stream's RM writings and publications. Members need time for discussions in small groups where they can ask questions and learn from each other, employing their God-given gifts. Also, much would be gained if church leaders were encouraged, as is *expected* by most denominations, to receive some theological teaching and training. Spiritual disciplines help shape the culture for spiritual formation. While spiritual disciplines are needed for transformation, Christians raised with the pattern hermeneutic can easily view disciplines as something more to add to what they do or believe. Thus, disciplines that seek to empty oneself such as solitude, spiritual retreats, and meditation can be helpful, but these must be taught. Conversational prayer and reflective readings that encourage one to listen to God's Spirit help adjust the pattern lens to longer range, multi-dimensional views.

Several initiatives have recently started to build unity within the RM churches, such as "Common Grounds Unity," with the mantra "unity begins with a cup of coffee."[319] These are local gatherings between the different streams for conversations meant to build unity. When meeting with those outside of one's own church, things that can be agreed upon should be acknowledged and celebrated. Groups can be encouraged to have worship nights of singing and prayer together, as many in the different streams know the same songs. Few things unite more than serving together, so serving should be a priority.

Churches should be encouraged to provide a safe place for members to bring their questions to the table without fear. With the pattern hermeneutic as our background, off-pattern questions have not often been welcomed, and those asking and exploring questions can feel judged. This method of interpretation built deep roots that are not easily dislodged. Legalistic perfectionism in interpretation implants in one's mind, thus affecting their personal peace and unity with others.

Jesus' life, death, and resurrection must remain the focal point in our Bible studies and worship, thus Acts becomes the result of the Gospels, instead of the gospel. We need teaching on the triune God to deepen the understanding of unity. Relationships deepen when the theology of the Trinity becomes normalized. Without this understanding, unity remains vague. The triune

---

319. Commongroundsunity.org

nature of God is seldom mentioned in our fellowship. Vocabulary that includes the Father, Son, and the Spirit can lead toward this becoming normative teaching. Vocabulary matters.

Teachings on the Spirit of God and deepening one's experiences of God should be encouraged, including spiritual disciplines (and God forbid,)[320] even liturgy that contributes to filling this gap. Humility and dependence on the leading of the Spirit must go beyond devotional thoughts and an opening prayer in leaders' meetings, and exhibit a deep dependence for the discernment from the Spirit over human knowledge, strategies, and efforts.

Leonard Allen, noting the importance of reason and certainty within our churches, describes the current communal worship and offers an alternative "...the role of the congregation is to sit and listen, but not to take part in or be swept away by the all-consuming Presence of God."[321] He offers an image of the future that envisions the church as a communion. He sees beyond the meaning of the Lord's Supper, but a communion that includes preaching and sharing the word, song, prayer, and each person using their gifts so that each person becomes the beneficiary of all the gifts. Members, as they participate in each other's lives, participate in the "very Life of God," as prayer and devotion accompany that Presence.[322]

Of great importance, there must be instilled a thirst for unity in our churches. This thirst must continue, and especially continue, when people, including church leaders, disagree, and especially when they disagree.

Perhaps the greatest measurement of spiritual formation can be summed in the love and unity expressed between Christians. Some would seek to call down fire from heaven on those who disagree with them, while others hope that further transformation into the image of Christ will result in deep-felt unity by which the world can know that they are disciples, by their love for one another (John 4:24).

---

320. I write this in jest, as liturgy has been taught in the RM as something to be avoided.

321. Allen, *Participating in God's Life*, 78.

322. Allen, *Participating in God's Life*, 79-80.

If unity without uniformity could be accepted as an asset instead of a need for separation, Jesus' prayer could become imagined in our churches. As Alex Pentland observes, "Sound quantitative and qualitative research clearly suggests that diversity is an asset, though our siloing behavior often directly contradicts these findings.[323] Such a new view of diversity in the RM requires intentional reflection and teaching, and much prayer.

Conclusion

I began this book arguing that our RM is rooted in patternism, which significantly affects formation and unity among our members. If we do not explore these roots, we can never expect to understand weaknesses and make needed changes. Restoration Movement church members have been taught that our church history began at Pentecost. This is misleading at best. We have been taught that other groups have founders, but we do not. This is false. In the ICOC, our history notes that we began in 1979 with a group of "thirty would-be disciples" in a living room, as if history before this date bore little significance to "God's modern-day movement," as we called ourselves. This misinformation needs to be clarified. History matters, but ours remains untaught or misconstrued. The teachings, hermeneutics, and forming tendencies of the RM's historical leaders and recent ICOC leaders I have explored show that our history and hermeneutic greatly influence our forming tendencies.

When I began to learn the missing pieces in my understanding of United States history, my new awareness helped change my heart toward the deeply engrained systemic racism in our country. Because most of our members have had little to no teaching on RM history nor any understanding of the default pattern hermeneutic, awareness of their forming tendencies remain overlooked and lacking. Most RM church members have been taught that we see scriptures correctly and others do not. This hermeneutic has

---

323. From a public lecture at Dominican University of California, Feb 5, 2014 as referenced in Alex Pentland, *Social Physics: How Good Ideas Spread* (New York: Penguin, 2014) and quoted in Liebert, *The Soul of Discernment,* 110.

and continues to have profound effects on spiritual formation and hinders the ability to be united with anyone who sees a pattern, example, or inference differently. While false teachings[324] have always existed and will continue to exist, patternism often strains at gnats and swallows camels. This mindset leaves little room for humble discussion or for unity in diversity.

We must become a church that intentionally acknowledges and teaches our history so that we can better understand our ways. We need teaching about ways we have interpreted Scripture to better acknowledge and teach the strengths, weaknesses, and forming tendencies of our default pattern hermeneutic. When we intentionally adjust the lens of patternism, we can become more readily formed into the image of Christ. Our churches need to better understand the theological and redemptive story of the Scriptures as we more intentionally engage and experience the Spirit of God in our interpretation. If we do not recognize and better understand our history and hermeneutic, change remains difficult. As James Baldwin famously noted, we cannot change what we do not face.

Can a hermeneutic that has such deep undergirdings within the RM be adjusted? I am tempted to throw up my hands and wave a flag of surrender. But then, I remember that the Spirit does what we cannot do. I share the words of Soeren:

> It's critical to say upfront that this transformation we seek is a gift to be received by our active God, not a technique to be mastered by driven people. Our future will hinge on this reality. Renewal movements throughout church history have always been led by ordinary people who are so desperate for change that they forfeit their capacity to make it happen in their own power. If we become the kind of people who simultaneously pray and hope desperately for change while refusing to control the outcomes, we will be astounded at what we get to experience.[325]

---

324. Most false teachings in the Scriptures concern pagan idolatry, Gnosticism, denying the resurrection, and legalism.

325. Tim Soerens, *Everywhere You Look: Discovering the Church Right Where You Are* (Downers Grove, IL: InterVarsity Press, 2020), 19.

The plea that rang out from early RM leaders remains a noble goal. Only through spiritual transformation into the image of Christ can this goal be achieved. Unity can never be achieved through a pattern interpretation of Scripture. New lenses must cut through presuppositions and fears to include the biblical narrative of God's love, His redemption, the trajectory of His aim, and the power of the Spirit as we learn to draw close to the heart of God, experiencing Him. As Christians draw close to Him, they come close to each other. As sectarian postures are exchanged for love for God that encompasses the essence of one's being in heart, mind, soul, and strength and love for neighbor as one's self, Jesus will be lifted up so that others are drawn to Him, including the next generation.

Jesus' last recorded prayer for unity has yet to be fulfilled. My prayer is that through greater clarity from revised lenses and dependence on the Spirit of God, we will be increasingly transformed into His likeness, finding our way toward that unity. As the "second touch" of Jesus allowed the blind man to see people instead of trees, perhaps a "second touch" from Jesus can also refine our lenses. As we view from clearer lenses, I pray that the "trees" we first see can lead us toward greater unity among others in the "Christian Forest." Even trees know how to participate in an intertwined, interdependent, and interworking community beneath the surface of what we see.[326] And, through a natural phenomenon known as inosculation,[327] two different trees, often but not always of the same species, graft and grow together. As the bark weakens, wears away, and the tree touches another tree, the trees begin to naturally unite, sharing nutrients and creating spectacular forest formations.

If trees of varied species can find unity in the forest, how much more should we, as those created in the image of God, experience unity as we are formed into the image of Christ? May we practice humility and vulnerability toward others that breed

---

326. Peter Wohlleben, *The Hidden Life of Trees: What They Feel, How They Communicate; Discoveries from a Secret World* (Vancouver: Greystone Books, 2016).

327. This word comes from a Latin term meaning "kiss" or "unite."

unity, thus forming spectacular reflections of the Lord. Then, Isaiah's words (Is. 55:12) can ring true today as the Living Word accomplishes God's desire and the purpose for which it was sent, and the mountains and hills burst into song while all the trees of the fields clap their hands.

328

328. Illustration by Cartoonstock.com

Bibliography

Abraham, William. *The Divine Inspiration of Holy Scripture.* Oxford: Oxford Univ Press, 1981.

------*The Logic of Renewal.* Grand Rapids, MI: Wm. B. Eerdmans, 2003.

Albritton, Travis, and Rodriguez, Corina. "The Art of Biblical Interpretation. Women and the Bible Podcast." Episode 6. https://www.audible.com/pd/6-The-Art-of-Biblical-Interpre-tation-Podcast/B09HSQ5D93?ref=a_pd_item-n_c0_lAsin_0_6&pf_rd_p=1da7ab30-c785-4a0e-a160-4a7e7077b353&pf_rd_r=2A9ZVNKS32F4SJJD4YC3.

Allen, Leonard. *Poured Out: The Spirit of God Empowering the Mission of God.* Abilene, TX: Abilene Christian University Press, 2018.

Allen, C. Leonard and Swick, Danny Gray. *Participating in God's Life: Two Crossroads for Churches of Christ.* Abilene, TX: Leafwood Publishers, 2001.

Bartholemew, Craig G. and Goheen, Michael W. *The Drama of Scripture: Finding Our Place in the Biblical Story.* Grand Rapids, MI: Baker Academic, 2014.

Barton, Ruth Haley. *Pursuing God's Will Together: A Discernment Practice for Leadership Groups.* Westmont, IL: IVP, 2012.

------*Strengthening the Soul of Your Leadership: Seeking God in the Crucible of Miinstry.* Westmont, IL: InterVarsity Press, 2018.

Blackaby, Henry and Richard, King, Claude. *Experiencing God: Knowing and Doing the Will of God.* Nashville, TN: LifeWay Press, 2007.

Borg, Marcus. *The Heart of Christianity.* NY: Harper Collins, 2003.

Borgo, Lacy Finn. *Spiritual Conversations with Children: Listening to God Together.* Westmont, IL: IVP, 2020.

Brauch, Manfred. *Abusing Scripture: The Consequences of Misreading the Bible.* Westmont, IL: IVP Academic, 2009.

Brown, Brené. *Atlas of the Heart: Mapping Meaningful Connection and the Language of Human Experience.* NY: Random House, 2021. Kindle edition.

Brown, Francis, Driver, S.R. and Briggs, C. A. *A Hebrew and English Lexicon of the Old Testament.* Oxford: Clarendon, 1976.

Brownlow, Leroy. *Why Am I Member of the Church of Christ, 57th printing,* Ft. Worth, TX: The Brownlow Corporation, 2008.

Burke, Gary PhD. *God's Woman Revisited*. Eugene, OR: Luminaire Press, 2017.

Campbell, Alexander. "A Restoration of the Ancient Order of Things, No. I. " *The Christian Baptist*, Vol. 2, No. 7. (1825). https://webfiles.acu.edu/departments/Library/HR/rest mov_nov11/www.mun.ca/rels/restmov/texts/acampbell/tcb/TCB207.HTM#Essay2.

------"Letters to an Independent Baptist." *Christian Baptist*, Vol. 3, No. 10. (May 1, 1826). https://webfiles.acu.edu/departments/Library/HR/restmov_nov11/www.mun.ca/rels/ restmov/texts/acampbell/tcb/TCB310.HTM.

------ "Preface," *Millennial Harbinger*, N.S. 3. (January 1839).

------ "Replication No. II to Spencer Clack." *Christian Baptist*, 5.2. (September 3, 1827). 370. https://webfiles.acu.edu/departments/Library/HR/restmov_nov11/www.mun.ca/ rels/restmov/texts/acampbell/tcb/TCB502.HTM#Essay5.

------"Schools and Colleges—No. II" *Millennial Harbinger* 3rd ser. 7. (March, 1850).

------"Slavery and the Fugitive Slave Law-No. II," *Millennial Harbinger*. (May, 1851).

------*The Christian System, in Reference to the Union of Christians and a Restoration of Primitive Christianity, as Pleaded in the Current Reformation*. London: Simpkin, Marshall and Co. 1843. Accessed July 12, 2023. https://webfiles.acu.edu/departments/Library/HR/ restmov_nov11/www.mun.ca/ rels/restmov/texts/acampbell/tcs2/TCS200A.HTM.

------"The Voice of God and the Word of God," *Millennial Harbinger*, Vol 1. (1830).

Carrillo, Robert. MDiv. ICOC church leader, former CEO HOPE worldwide, ICOC teacher. Interview on October 20, 2022.

Chan, Francis. *Until Unity*. Colorado Springs, CO: David C. Cooke. 2012.

Chan, Francis and Yankoski, Danae. *Forgotten God: Reversing Our Tragic Neglect of the Holy Spirit*. Colorado Springs, CO: David Cook, 2009.

Chan, Sam. *Evangelism in a Skeptical World: How to Make the Unbelievable News about Jesus More Believable*. Grand Rapids, MI. Zondervan, 2018.

Childers, Jeff W., Douglas A. Foster, Jack R. Reese. *The Crux of the Matter: Crisis, Tradition, and the Future of Churches of Christ*. Abilene Christian University Press, 2002.

Chole, Alicia Britt. *40 Days of Decrease: A Different Kind of Hunger. A Different Kind of Fast*. Nashville, TN: W Publishing, 2016.

Claiborne, Shane, Wilson-Hartgrove, Jonathan, Okoro, Enuma. *Common Prayer: A Liturgy for Ordinary Radicals*. Grand Rapids, MI: Zondervan, 2010.

Codgill, Roy E. "That Arlington Meeting," *Gospel Guardian*, vol 20, no. 17. nd. http://articles.ochristian.com/article15449.shtml.

Cope, James R. "Biblical Authority: Its Meaning and Application." *Florida College Annual Lectures.* Temple Terrace FL, 1974.

------*Walking by Faith, 10th ed.* Bowling Green, KY: Guardian of Truth Foundation. 1984. https://www.restorationlibrary.org/library/WBF/WBF_SIPDF.pdf.

------*The New Testament Church.* Cogdill Foundation, 21st Edition, 1979, http://www.biblestudyguide.org/ebooks/cogdill/n-t-church-cogdill.PDF.

De Long, Kindalee Pfremmer. "Reading Luke's Story of Jesus and the Way." *Teleios: A Journal to Promote Holitic Christian Spirituality.* Vol. 5. No. 1, 2023.

"Disciples Today" disciplestoday.org.

Draper, James. *Authority: The Critical Issue for Southern Baptists*. Old Tappan, NJ: Revell, 1984.

East, Brad. *The Church's Book: Theology of Scripture in Ecclesial Context.* Grand Rapids, MI: Eerdmans, 2002.

Enns, Peter. *The Sin of Certainty: Why God Desires Our Trust More than our "Correct" Beliefs.* San Francisco, CA: Harper One, 2016.

Errett, Isaac. "Our Position." *The Standard.* http://articles.ochristian.com/article15449.shtml.

Evans, Rachel Held. *Inspired: Slaying Giants, Walking on Water, and Loving the Bible Again.* Nashville, TN: Thomas Nelson, 2018.

------*Searching for Sundays: Loving, Leaving, and Finding the Church.* Nashville, TN: Nelson, 2015.

Fee, Gordon. *Listening to the Spirit in the Text.* Grand Rapids, MI: Eerdmans-Lightning Source, 2000.

Ferguson, Gordon. Author, teacher, and former director of the Pacific School of Ministry. Interview on November 4, 2022.

Ferguson, Gordon. *My Three Lives: A Story of One Man and Three Movements.* Spring, TX: Illumination Publishers, 2016.

Fleming, Andrew C. "Let Each One Be Careful How He Builds: A Study of the Statistical Narrative of the International Churches of Christ," 2018. Unpublished paper. Kiev, Ukraine, April 2018. missionstory.com. https://www.archive.missionstory.com/ICOC_Culture_and_Narrative_Articles/let-each-one-be-careful-how-he-builds-(2018).html.

Foster, Douglas. *A Life of Alexander Campbell*. Grand Rapids, MI: Eerdmans, 2020.

------"An Essay on Unity." Dec 5, 2020. https://www.douglasjacoby.com/a-unity-essay-by-douglas-a-foster/.

------"The Stone-Campbell Movement and the International Church of Christ: What Has the ICOC Contributed to the SCM, and What Does the ICOC Need to Hear?" *Teleios: A Journal to Promote Holistic Christian Spirituality*. Vol 1. No 2. New York: Crossroad Publishing, 2021.

Foster, Douglas, Blowers, Paul, Dunnavant, Anthony, Williams, D. Newell. *The Encyclopedia of the Stone-Campbell Movement*. Grand Rapids, MI: Eerdmans, 2012.

Foster, Richard. *Streams of Living Water: Essential Practices From the Six Great Traditions of Christian Faith*. San Francisco, CA: Harper, 2001.

Gengler, Michael T. *We Can Do It: A Community Takes on the Challenge of School Desegregation*. New York: Rosetta Books, 2018.

Giles, Glenn PhD. "Intimate, Positive, Experiential, Relationship as the Focal Point or Organizational Center and Impetus for the Bible sustained by Yada'/Ginosko Theology: An Inquiry." a paper presented at the ICOC Teachers Conference on The Art of Scripture Reading. Feb 25, 2022.

Guin, Jay. "The Blue Parakeet Corollaries – Positive Law." Blog, *One in Jesus*. May 18, 2009. http://oneinjesus.info/2009/05/the-blue-parakeet-corollaries-positive-law/.

Guinness, Os. *The Call: Finding and Fulfilling God's Purpose for Your Life*. Nashville, TN: W Publishing, 2018.

Guyon, Madame Jean. *A Short and Easy Method of Prayer: Discovering Peace and Intimacy Through Fellowship With God*. Apollo, PA: Ichthus, 1875.

Hardeman, N.B. "Hardeman's Tabernacle Sermons: Vol 1." March 28-April 16, 1922.

Harding, James A. "Prayer for the Sick." *The Way* 3.6. 9 May, 1901.

Harris, Laird R., Archer Jr., Gleason L, and Waltke, Bruce K. Waltke. *Theological Wordbook of the Old Testament*. Vol 1. Chicago: Moody, 1980.

Heschel, Abraham Joshua. *The Sabbath*. New York: Farrar, Straus, and Giroux, 1951.

Hicks, John Mark. *Searching for the Pattern: My Journey in Interpreting the Bible*. Nashville, TN: John Mark Hicks, 2019.

------Blog, May 31, 2008. https://johnmarkhicks.com/2008/05/31/stone-campbell-hermeneutics-v-moral-and-positive-law/.

------"Recentering: My Theological Journey in Churches of Christ." *Teleios: A Journal to Promote Holistic Christian Spirituality*. Vol 1. No 2. New York: Crossroad Publishing, 2021.

------"Searching for the Pattern" *Teleios: A Journal to Promote Holistic Christian Spirituality.* Vol. 5. No. 1. Chestnut Ridge, NY: Crossroad Publishing, 2022.

------*Women Serving God.* Nashville: John Mark Hicks, 2020.

Hobbes, Thomas. *Leviathan.* Oxford, UK: Oxford University Press, 2009.

Hougen, Judith. *Transformed into Fire: Discovering Your True Identity as God's Beloved.* Grand Rapids, MI: Kregel, 2009.

Hughes, Richard. *Reviving the Ancient Faith: The History of Churches of Christ in America.* Abilene, TX: Abilene Christian University Press, 1996.

icochistory.org

Jacobs, Alan. *The Theology of Reading: The Hermeneutics of Love.* Boulder, CO: Westview, 2001.

Jacoby, Douglas.MTS, DMin, IBTM, T&R, AIM, Professor of Theology, Rocky Mountain School of Ministry and Theology and Adjunct Professor, Lincoln University. Interview on October 18, 2022.

Jennings, Timothy R. MD. *The God Shaped Brain: How Changing Your View of God Transforms Your Life.* Downers Grove, IL: IVP Books, 2017.

Johnston, William, ed. *The Cloud of Unknowing: And The Book of Privy Counseling.* New York: Doubleday, 1973.

Jones, Thomas A. Author, teacher, and former editor "Discipleship Publications International." Interview on October 26, 2022.

------*In Search of a City: An Autobiographical Perspective on a Remarkable but Controversial Movement.* Billerica, MA: DPI, 2007.

Keener, Craig. *Spirit Hermeneutics: Reading Scripture in Light of Pentecost.* Grand Rapids, MI: Eerdmans, 2016.

Kinder, Donald M. *Capturing Head to Heart: The Lives of Early Popular Stone-Campbell Movement Leaders.* Abilene, TX: Abilene Christian University Press. Kindle Edition, 2012.

Kinnard, Steve, ed. *Teleios: A Journal to Promote Holistic Christian Spirituality,* Vol 1. Chestnut Ridge, NY: Crossroads Publishing, 2021.

------*Teleios: A Journal to Promote Holistic Christian Spirituality,* Vol 2. Chestnut Ridge, NY: Crossroads Publishing, 2021.

Klingman, George A. *Church History for Busy People.* Denver, CO: Armory Publishing, 2019.

Kosuke, Koyama. *Three Mile an Hour God*. London, UK: SCM Press, 2021.

Kriete, Henry. "Honest to God: Revolution through Repentance and freedom in Christ." DouglasJacoby.com: Articles. 2 Feb., 2003 [online]; accessed 11 Feb 2013; available from http:// douglasjacoby.com/articles/1511-honest-to-god-by-henry-kriete.

Langberg, Diane. *Redeeming Power*. Grand Rapids, MI: Baker Publishing. 2020. Kindle edition.

Levison, Jack. *Fresh Air: The Holy Spirit for an Inspired Life*. Brewster, MA: Paraclete Press, 2012.

Lewis, C.S. *The Weight of Glory*. New York: Harper One, 1976.

Liebert, Elizabeth. *The Soul of Discernment: A Spiritual Practice for Communities and Institutions*. Louisville, KY: Westminster John Knox Press, 2015.

Lipscomb, David. "Tolbert Fanning's Teaching and Influence" in James Scobey. *Franklin College and Its Influences* 1906; reprint. Nashville: *Gospel Advocate*, 1954.

Love, Mark. "Reading Scripture On Its Own Terms." *Teleios: A Journal to Promote Holistic Christian Spirituality*. Vol. 5. No. 1. Chestnut Ridge, NY: Crossroad Publishing, 2022.

Luhrmann, T.M. *How God Becomes Real: Kindling the Presence of Invisible Others*. Princeton, NJ: Princeton University Press, 2020.

Martin, James. *The Jesuit Guide to (Almost) Everything: A Spirituality for Real Life*. San Francisco: Harper One, 2012.

McKean, Kip, "Revolution Through Restoration," all volumes. http://www.usd21.org/wp-content/uploads/2012/06/Revolution _Through_Restoration.pdf (accessed November 14, 2022).

McKnight, Scot. *Open to the Spirit: God in Us, God With Us, God Transforming Us*. NY: Waterbrook, 2018.

------*The Blue Parakeet: Rethinking How You Read the Bible*. Grand Rapids, MI: Zondervan, 2018.

Migliore, Daniel L. *Faith Seeking Understanding: An Introduction to Christian Theology*. Grand Rapids, MI: Eerdmans, 2004.

Moore, William Thomas. *Comprehensive History of Disciples of Christ*. NY: Fleming H Revell, 1909.

Mulholland, M. Robert Jr. *Shaped by the Word: The Power of Scripture in Spiritual Formation*. Nashville, TN: Upper Room, 2001.

Murch, James DeForest, *Christians Only: A History of the Restoration Movement.* Cincinatti, OH: Standard Publishing, 2004.

Newberg, Andrew and Waldman, Mark Robert. *How God Changes Your Brain: Breakthrough Findings from a Leading Neurologist.* New York: Random House, 2009.

Newbigin, Leslie. *Foolishness to the Greeks: The Gospel and Western Culture.* Grand Rapids, MI: Eerdmans, 1986.

Newland, Wayne. *Book, Chapter, and Paragraph: Restoring Context.* Falmouth, ME: Heritage Books, 2010.

Noll, Austin. *A Jumble of Crumpled Papers: A Church Kid's Journey from Confidence, to Questioning, to Christ.* Wise Path Books, 2021. Kindle.

Nouwen, Henri, with Christenson, Michael, and Laird, Rebecca. *Spiritual Direction: Wisdom for the Long Walk of Faith.* NY: HarperOne, 2006.

Nouwen, J.M. Nouwen. *In the Name of Jesus: Reflections on Christian Leadership.* New York: Crossroad Publishing, 2002

------*Life of the Beloved: Spiritual Living in a Secular World.* NY: Crossroad, 1992.

------*Spiritual Formation: Following the Movements of the Spirit.* NY: HarperOne, 2010.

O'Connell-Rodwell, Caitlin E. "Keeping an 'Ear' to the Ground: Seismic Communication in Elephants." *American Physiological Society Journal.* August 1, 2007. https://doi.org/10.1152/physiol.00008, 2007.

Olbricht, Thomas. *Hearing God's Voice: My Life with Scripture in the Churches of Christ.* Abilene, TX: ACU Press, 1996.

------"Hermeneutics in Churches of Christ." *Restoration Quarterly 37,* No 1, 1995.

Oxford Handbooks Online. https://www.oxfordhandbooks.com/view/10.1093/oxfordhb/9780199234097.001.0001/oxfordhb-9780199234097-e-3.

Paquette, Jonah PsyD. *Awestruck: How Embracing Wonder Can Make You Happier, Healthier, and More Connected.* Boulder, CO: Shambhala, 2020.

Pennington, Basil. *Centering Prayer.* NY: Image, 1980.

Pinnock, Clark. *Flame of Love: A Theology of the Holy Spirit.* Downers Grove, IL: Intervarsity, 1996.

Pocta, David. "Thomas Wayne McKean: Saint or Scoundrel—Normalizing Extreme Perspectives on a Foundational Figure in the International Church of Christ." *Teleios: A Journal to Promote Christian Spirituality,* Vol 1, No 2. NY: Crossroad Publishing, 2021.

Pocta, David, PhD. Director of DCE (Disciples Center for Education), Director, Institute for the Study of Contemporary Spirituality, Oblate School of Theology. Zoom Interview on October 12, 2022.

Poling, James and Miller, Donald E. *Foundations For a Practical Theology of Ministry.* Nashville, TN: Abingdon Press, 2000.

Reese, Jack. *At the Blue Hole: Elegy for a Church on the Edge.* Grand Rapids, MI. Eerdmans, 2021.

Richardson, Robert. *Memoirs of Alexander Campbell* vol 2. Indianapolis, IN: Religious Book Service, 2018.

Rolheiser, Ron. "Teaching and Spirituality." *Teleios: A Journal to Promote Holistic Spirituality,* Vol 1, No 5. Chestnut Ridge, NY: Crossroad Publishing, 2022.

Root, Andrew. *Faith Formation in a Secular Age.* Grand Rapids: MI: Baker Academic, 2017.

------*The Congregation in a Secular Age: Keeping Sacred Time Against the Speed of Modern Life.* Ada, MI: Baker Academic, 2021.

Sanders, Oswald. *My Utmost for His Highest.* Grand Rapids MI: Daily Bread, 2017.

Santos, Gabriel. "Dopamine Hits, Tweets, and Rage: Hermeneutics for Peacemakers." *Teleios: A Journal to Promote Holistic Christian Spirituality.* Vol. 5. No. 1. Chestnut Ridge, NY: Crossroad Publishing, 2022.

Shaw, Jeanie. *The View from Paul's Window: Paul's Teachings on Women.* Spring, TX: Illumination Publishers, 2020.

Shelly, Rubel. *I Just Want to Be a Christian.* Nashville, TN: 20th Century Christian, 1986.

Simpson-Cabelin, Shari. Author, Disney Screenwriter. ICOC lay leader. Interview on November 3, 2022.

Smith, F. LaGard, *The Cultural Church: Winds of Change and the Call for a "New Hermeneutic."* Nashville, TN: 20th Century Christian, 1992.

Smith, James Bryan. *The Good and Beautiful God: Falling in Love with the God Jesus Knows.* Downers Grove, IL: IVP Books, 2009.

Soerens, Tim, *Everywhere You Look: Discovering the Church Right Where You Are.* Downers Grove, IL: Intervarsity Press, 2020.

Solomon, Marty. *Asking Better Questions of the Bible: A Guide for the Wounded, Weary & Longing for More.* Colorado Springs, CO: NavPress, 2023.

Stanback, Foster, *Into All Nations: A History of the International Churches of Christ.* Spring,

TX: Illumination Publishers, 2005.

Staten, Steve. Organizational health consultant, trainer, teacher. Interview on October 11, 2022.

Stone, Barton. "The Retrospect." *Christian Messenger.* 7 October, 1833

------"Remarks." *Christian Messenger.* August, 1835.

Susek, Ron, *Firestorm: Preventing and Overcoming Church Conflicts.* Ada, MI: Baker, 1999.

Takle, David. Forming: *A Work of Grace.* USA: Kingdom Formation Ministries, 2012, 2013, 2021.

The Sacred Censer. "Trisagion Films." Dec 17, 2014. https://www.youtube.com/watch?v=Ialuqt-bZXs&list=RDLVIaluqt-bZXs.

Thomas, J.D. *We Be Brethren: A Study in Biblical Interpretation.* Whitefish, MT: Literary Licensing LLC, 2011.

Tippens, Darryl. *Pilgrim Heart: The Way of Jesus in Everyday Life.* Abilene, TX: Leafwood Press, 2006.

Tozer, A.W. *God's Pursuit of Man: Tozer's Profound Prequel to the Pursuit of God.* Chicago: Moody Publishers. 1950, 1978.

Wallace, Daniel B. and Sawyer, M. James, eds. *Who's Afraid of the Holy Spirit?: An Investigation into the Ministry of the Spirit of God Today.* Dallas: Biblical Studies Press, 2013.

Waters, Lanelle. *The One Another Way.* Gainesville, FL: Crossroads Publications, 1979.

Webb, William J. Slaves, *Women, and Homosexuals: Exploring the Hermeneutics of Cultural Analysis.* Downers Grove, IL: IVP Academic, 2001.

Wharton, Edward C. *The Church of Christ: A Presentation of the Distinctive Nature and Identity of the New Testament Church.* West Monroe, LA: Howard Book House, 1970.

Wilkins, Jen. *Women of the Word: How to Study the Bible with Both our Hearts and Minds.* Wheaton, IL: Crossway, 2014.

Willard, Dallas, *Renovation of the Heart: Putting on the Character of Christ.* Colorado Springs, CO: NavPress, 2002.

Williams, D. Newell. *Barton Stone: A Spiritual Biography.* St. Louis, MO: Chalice Press, 2000.

Wohlleben, Peter. *The Hidden Life of Trees: What They Feel, How They Communicate— Discoveries from a Secret World.* Vancouver: Greystone Books, 2016.

Woodruff, James. *The Church in Transition*. Searcy, AR: The Bible House, 1990.

Wright, N.T. *Paul for Everyone: The Prison Letters: Ephesians, Philippians, Colossians, and Philemon 2nd ed*. Louisville, KY: Westminster John Knox, 2004.

------*The Last Word: Scripture and the Authority of God-Getting Beyond the Bible Wars*. San Francisco, CA. Harper One, 2006.

------*Surprised by Scripture: Engaging Contemporary Issues*. San Francisco, CA: Harper One, 2015.

Yancey, Philip. *The Jesus I Never Knew*. Grand Rapids, MI: Zondervan, 1995.

------*Where the Light Fell: A Memoir*. Colorado Springs, CO: Convergent Books, 2021.

Books by Jeanie Shaw

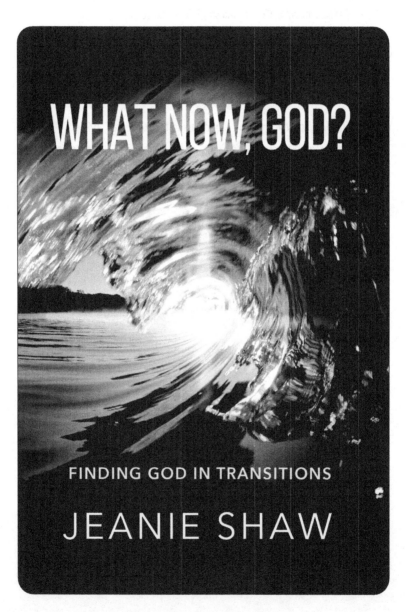

WHAT NOW, GOD?

FINDING GOD IN TRANSITIONS

JEANIE SHAW

Available at www.ipibooks.com and Amazon.com

Jeanie Shaw

Every
Day
Is A
New
Chance

Available at www.ipibooks.com and Amazon.com

Jeanie Shaw & Friends
An Aging Grace

My Morning Cup
And Other Spiritual Thoughts

Jeanie Shaw

Available at www.ipibooks.com and Amazon.com

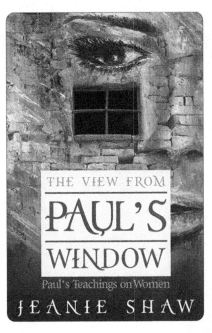

THE VIEW FROM

PAUL'S
WINDOW

Paul's Teachings on Women

JEANIE SHAW

Jeanie Shaw and Friends

The
Sacred
Journey

Finding God
in Caregiving

Available at www.ipibooks.com and Amazon.com

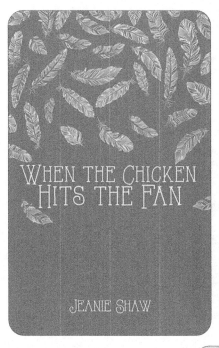

WHEN THE CHICKEN
HITS THE FAN

JEANIE SHAW

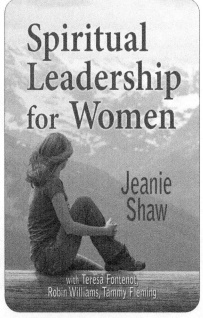

Spiritual
Leadership
for Women

Jeanie
Shaw

with Teresa Fontenot,
Robin Williams, Tammy Fleming

Available at www.ipibooks.com and Amazon.com

Made in United States
North Haven, CT
16 July 2024